W9-ABN-305

At Issue

Do Religious Groups in America Experience Discrimination?

Other Books in the At Issue series:

At Issue

Do Religious Groups in America Experience Discrimination?

Janel Ginn, Book Editor

GREENHAVEN PRESS

An imprint of Thomson Gale, a part of The Thomson Corporation

Detroit • New York • San Francisco • New Haven, Conn. • Waterville, Maine • London

Christine Nasso, *Publisher*
Elizabeth Des Chenes, *Managing Editor*

© 2007 Thomson Gale, a part of The Thomson Corporation.

Thomson and Star logo are trademarks and Gale and Greenhaven Press are registered trademarks used herein under license.

For more information, contact:
Greenhaven Press
27500 Drake Rd.
Farmington Hills, MI 48331-3535
Or you can visit our Internet site at http://www.gale.com

LIBRARY OF CONGRESS CATALOGING-IN-PUBLICATION DATA

Do religious groups In America experience discrimination? / Janel Ginn, book editor.
    p. cm. -- (At issue)
    Includes bibliographical references and index.
    ISBN-13: 978-0-7377-3399-0 (hardcover)
    ISBN-10: 0-7377-3399-3 (hardcover)
    ISBN-13: 978-0-7377-3400-3 (pbk.)
    ISBN-10: 0-7377-3400-0 (pbk.)
    1. Freedom of religion--United States. 2. Discrimination--Religious aspects.
3. Discrimination--United States. 4. Prejudices. 5. Civil rights--United States.
I. Ginn, Janel, 1983-
    BL640.D6 2007
    305.60973--dc22
                                                            2006038935

Printed in the United States of America
10 9 8 7 6 5 4 3 2 1

Contents

Introduction

The U.S. Constitution protects freedom of religion, but does that guarantee religious groups protection from discrimination? Recently, the question seems to be more debatable than ever. With allegations of Muslims in America facing persecution following the terrorist attacks of September 11, 2001, and numerous court cases against professing Christians for violating the separation between church and state, freedom of religion and freedom from religion are difficult to separate.

In 2002, atheist Michael Newdow brought a case before the 9th Circuit Court of Appeals. He sued on behalf of his daughter to remove the words "under God" from the Pledge of Allegiance, which violated Newdow's belief system. The U.S. Justice Department immediately filed an appeal to reverse the court's decision. The U.S. Supreme Court agreed to hear the case in 2004, but determined that because Michael Newdow did not have custody of his daughter, he could not sue on her behalf. The case was dismissed, but it sparked a debate from individual households to the highest levels of government.

The balance between the First Amendment and the idea of separation of church and state has been a topic of debate since the founding of the United States. But in an age where the number of religions represented among Americans is growing, and people who want no affiliation with religion whatsoever become more vocal about their discontentment, the topic is now a controversial issue.

Proponents on both sides of the argument have strong feelings. Those whose religious convictions are integral to their way of life demand that their freedoms should be protected as guaranteed by the First Amendment and the Bill of Rights. They enjoy the opportunity to practice their religious traditions and publicly discuss their faith, and argue that if their freedom is infringed, the United States will be no different from countries where the government controls or outright abolishes the ability of citizens to follow the religious beliefs of their choice.

Those on the other side claim they do not want to restrict anyone's religious freedom, but they don't want their religious choice, or their decision to observe no faith, infringed upon either. They argue that by using the words "under God" in the Pledge of Allegiance or "In God We Trust" on American currency forces Americans who do not believe in or submit to the authority of any god to endorse a belief they do not possess.

The issue has been complicated in recent years by several events. Muslims claim they have experienced an increase in discrimination based on both race and religion following the terrorist attacks on September 11, 2001. Many Muslim women believe they are targeted for invasive and demeaning searches by airport security when they are seen wearing the clothing in adherence to the teachings of their religion. In addition to the court case filed with regard to the words "under God" in the Pledge of Allegiance, cases have been filed against praying in God's name at public school athletic events, Bible studies meeting on school grounds, and displays of religious holiday symbols such as menorahs or mangers on government property.

In addition, religious discrimination is becoming a problem within churches. A split among congregation members over traditional interpretation of scriptures and a modern view of tolerance has created rifts in several denominations, but perhaps most notably among Episcopalians, who are divided over the issue of placing homosexuals in positions of authority in the denomination.

When the framers of the Constitution protected religious freedom, the decision was motivated by the religious persecution many of them endured before coming to America. They wanted to ensure their descendants would not suffer for their beliefs. It is almost certain, however, they could not foresee the religious diversity now present in America or the ways the First Amendment would create controversy in the twenty-first century.

1

Christians Experience Discrimination in Schools

Toni Weingarten

Toni Weingarten is a contributing writer to the Christian Science Monitor.

At a time when the American education system encourages toler-ance and celebrates diversity more than ever, Christians find themselves victims of ridicule for their faith. Students claim that their beliefs are openly mocked in college classrooms around the country and the professors do not encourage the same respect be shown for their religion as every other belief system discussed in class.

When Chris Gruener moved to the San Francisco Bay Area to begin graduate school, he looked forward to ex-periencing the region's renowned tolerance of all people and lifestyles.

Mr. Gruener was raised in a devout Christian family near Seattle and attended a Baptist high school and a Christian col-lege, where he studied business. His passion, however, was lit-erature, and so he was excited to begin a master's program in English at Sonoma State University. But during his first se-mester, a classroom incident put a damper on Gruener's ar-dor.

While lecturing on [Irish writer] James Joyce's rejection of the church, a professor drew two mountains with a valley be-

Toni Weingarten, "Campus Christians: Not Always at Ease," *Christian Science Monitor*, vol. 97, January 25, 2005. Copyright 2005 The Christian Science Publishing Society. Reproduced by permission of the author.

tween them on the chalkboard, explaining that Joyce's church believed one mountain was man and the other mountain was God.

Next he drew a cross in the valley, touching both peaks—a visual metaphor Gruener knew from childhood—and explained that this was Christ on the cross connecting man to God. Then the professor broke into peals of mocking laughter. The rest of the class joined in.

"My heart stopped," says Gruener. "If this were any other religion, the professor wouldn't get away with his remarks—it would be politically incorrect. But in the Bay Area, it is OK to laugh at Christianity and its God."

Today, on college campuses throughout the United States, great stress is placed on the importance of treating divergent views with sensitivity. And there are many religious students who say they appreciate the respect with which their beliefs are received.

But today, it is just as likely to be America's majority faith group—Christians—who complain of discrimination or plead for more tolerance on campus.

Yet complaints like Gruener's are not uncommon and, ironically, they are sometimes heard at schools that particularly pride themselves on being open-minded and tolerant. Christians, from conservative to liberal, say that on a college campus they not infrequently experience overt disrespect—and sometimes even discrimination.

Liz Howlson, a senior majoring in American Cultures at the University of Michigan, is a member of the school's Inter-Varsity Christian Fellowship. In a religion class she took, she says, "They talked all about how Christianity has ruined so many things, and I kind of felt embarrassed to be a Christian."

Tension between faith and academics is, of course, nothing new. But the role of religion at US colleges and universities—many of which were originally founded by churches—has become more complicated over the past several decades as most schools have become more secular.

Changing Times

Once upon a time, it was primarily non-Christians who expressed concerns about religious discrimination. They faced the challenge of keeping their traditions in a Christian-centric environment, where their belief systems could easily be misunderstood or overlooked, and where exams might be scheduled during holy days such as Judaism's Yom Kippur or activities planned during Muslim prayer periods.

But today, it is just as likely to be America's majority faith group—Christians—who complain of discrimination or plead for more tolerance on campus.

"There's no way for diverging views [in classes] to be disclosed in an intelligent way," says Nika Elguardo, a devout Christian who, last year, completed a master's degree at Harvard University's Kennedy School of Government. She found the professors there generally very respectful of her religious views. But the students, she says, were another matter.

At Harvard, Ms. Elguardo says, secular humanism is the mainstream view. "There are ways of thinking that went against mainstream views . . . and students in class were shut down by others" when they expressed those views.

Ann Carter, a junior majoring in psychology at Sonoma State and a Christian active in her church, has also felt disrespected in class.

As a freshman, she took a "multiculturalism" class focused on debating topics as diverse as gun control, Hindu theology, and vegetarianism. Part of her grade rested on speaking up and sharing her views.

"I'd say God, and talk about Christ. People would laugh at me and [the professor] did nothing to stop it," says Ms. Carter. "But any other opinion at which students disagreed or laughed she'd stop the class and say, 'We need to be sensitive!'"

In a liberal stronghold like the Bay Area, Christians are often stereotyped, says the Rev. Adam Blons, a member of the University Religious Council at the University of California at Berkeley and head of that city's First Congregational Church. People are quick to assume that all Christians are humorless fundamentalists bent on converting others, he says. "I can confirm that it isn't easy to be 'out' as a Christian."

The Perceived Conflict between Faith and Reason

That experience is not limited to elite schools on the coasts.

"You find it at a lot of state universities," says Dan Myers, chairman of the Department of Sociology at Notre Dame University. "There's an issue, kind of ironic, that those who are attempting to be so open-minded are relatively close-minded about the religion piece of the thing."

Professor Myers attributes this attitude in part to overzealous Christians who tell others they are wrong not to accept Jesus. He also sees it as a reaction to religion's long history of suppressing free thought, though he says he experiences full academic freedom at his Catholic university.

Sometimes the very policies designed to respect diversity end up working against campus religious groups.

"My take is that Notre Dame has some confidence that its religious commitments can stand up to some scrutiny, challenges, and critical thinking," Myers says of the classes he teaches that cover both sides of the abortion and gay rights movements.

But that's not always the case at more secular schools, others charge.

"The attitude here is if you're of faith, then you are intellectually inferior," says Gruener.

Critical thinking is core to American higher education, says Edward Ochoa, provost and vice president of academic affairs at Sonoma State University. But so is the idea of the moral development of the young, a value inherited from the English tradition of religious colleges.

"What survives of the religious college model is the liberal arts paradigm of trying to develop the whole person, but it has become more secular," says Dr. Ochoa. He notes that the Sonoma professor who mocked religion is not the norm, and that his school—like most—has a policy of respecting diversity.

Religious Freedom Versus Discrimination

In a strange twist, however, sometimes the very policies designed to respect diversity end up working against campus religious groups.

"What you have is basically an institutionalized policy that says an organization that believes in certain absolutes that conflict with very broad nondiscrimination policy have no place on campus," says David French, president of the Foundation for Individual Rights in Education (FIRE) in Philadelphia, a nonprofit that defends academic freedom.

He cites a case brought to FIRE in 2000. A lesbian at Tufts University who'd long been a member of an InterVarsity-affiliated Christian group said she no longer agreed with the group's stand on sexual morality. Despite this, she wanted to be part of the group's leadership.

The group welcomed her as a member but said its leadership must share their core beliefs, in addition to meeting certain training requirements.

The woman filed a complaint with Tufts for religious and sexual discrimination and a student judicial panel threw the group off campus. The university administration, however, felt the decision had been hasty and asked for a review.

On review, the judicial panel ruled the woman had not met training requirements but also said the group exhibited sexual discrimination. The woman, independently, withdrew her complaint and the group had to rewrite its constitution, rephrasing its statements on sexuality.

Gay rights are a flash point on many campuses, often creating an awkward collision between ideals of religious freedom and charges of discrimination, says French.

When such cases arise, he adds, the response from college administrators is often "Oh, we had no idea that would infringe on First Amendment rights."

Bruce Reitman, dean of students at Tufts, disagrees. "It's a clash of values of two groups that we hold dearly," he says of school discomfort in being asked to choose between religious and gay rights.

FIRE acknowledges that a school has the right to take a stand and say that it dislikes a certain religious group's stand against homosexuality.

But he adds, "The problem we have is when the state, even secular liberal arts colleges, takes official action to extinguish that point of view and shut down the marketplace of ideas. The problem on campuses again and again is that the notion of religious liberty and free association must bow before the dominant ideology . . . and the dominant ideology is a particular brand of secularism . . . that says faith has no place at the table."

Minority religious groups file far fewer discrimination complaints with FIRE, says French. He speculates that these non-Christian groups are often deemed desirable on campuses eager to appear multicultural, and that it is the large size and prevalence of the Christian groups that lead to actions against them.

2

Anti-semitic Actions on Campus Are Unacceptable

Kenneth S. Stern

Kenneth S. Stern is an expert on anti-Semitism and bigotry for the American Jewish Committee. He is the author of three books, appears frequently on television news shows, and has spoken before the U.S. Court and Congress.

The discrimination Jews face on American campuses should not be tolerated. Disguising anti-Semitism under criticism of Israel's recent actions in defense of their land and citizens is unacceptable. When put to the bigotry test, colleges across the nation fail miserably. Criticism of Israel's actions is acceptable; blatantly discriminating against Jewish people is not.

My favorite grafitto was carved—not just penned—into the green wooden stall wall of a college men's room. It said, "If I didn't believe it with my own mind, I never would have seen it."

While this graffito appeared in the 1970s and may have been a comment on the drug culture, it remains a great definition of dogmatism. People may believe things so strongly that they twist what they think they see like a pretzel to conform to and confirm their a priori beliefs.

Bigotry that is ideologically inspired—which is bigotry at its most dangerous—always works by this rule. Beliefs define what is seen and what is not seen, and anything that cannot be distorted to support the set-in-stone premise is ignored or explained away. White supremacists, for example, can see only what whites have contributed to the building of America. Holocaust deniers, of course, will try to explain away gas chambers as air raid shelters or morgues, and don't consider the implications of their distortions: If they are correct, then the thousands of tenured professors who teach about the Holocaust and World War II, whether in the U.S., Britain, Germany, Israel, or elsewhere, are all incompetent, part of a grand conspiracy, or both.

This blinding bigotry is most distressing and perilous when practiced by otherwise intelligent and educated people. Many would like to believe that education is a sufficient antidote to bigotry, but the facts demonstrate otherwise. There have always been too many very well-educated bigots. Just ask the Southern blacks who were victimized, not only by the lynchings of the Ku Klux Klan in the 1950s and 1960s, but also by the powerful local white "citizens councils" that spoke about "states' rights" and whose members included many well-educated community leaders.

Today many educated bigots are active on American campuses. Some are promoting anti-Semitism in the guise of criticism of Israel.

Israel, of course, should not be immune from criticism, any more than any other country is. But too many complaints about Israel are unmistakably driven by anti-Semitism. The current divestiture and "boycott" movements are a case in point.

Bigotry 101: Identifying Bigotry

Consider "Bigotry-finder rule 101": Take a situation, change the race, religion, sexual orientation, or other aspect of the players' identities, and see if the same results apply.

I cited this test repeatedly in the aftermath of the Oklahoma City bombing, when white supremacists were the engine of the militia movement, but Congress refused to hold any serious investigation into the problem. I argued that if this same movement, with the same means and plans for acts of domestic terror, were being driven by thousands of black supremacists, members of Congress would have left skid marks racing to the podium to demand full-scale hearings. Congressional failure to do so was evidence of a double standard that had less to do with the nature of the threat than with the color of skin.

Similarly, the attacks on Israel on campus today reflect a double standard that can only be explained by bigotry, by the fact that Jews are in this "scenario."

Listen to the criticism of any other country: It is always a political party, a program, a policy, or a person that is criticized, never the legitimacy of a society. Except for Israel.

Even if a person is a revolutionary Marxist who sees both Israel and the United States as "settler colonialist imperialist" powers, how is it that he or she believes that the U.S. should be reorganized by revolution, but the Jewish state should disappear?

And even if a person believes that Israel's presence in the West Bank and Gaza is illegitimate, immoral and illegal, why is it that Israel is lambasted in sign after sign for the "occupation," when there were no similar signs just decades ago when Jordan and Egypt were in control of these same areas for nearly 20 years? And why are there no signs today lambasting Syria, which occupies Arab land in Lebanon, right next door?

The answer: Bigotry-finder rule 101. Take Jews out of this picture, and other rules apply.

Or consider another example: Some progressives compare Palestinians to American Indians and Israelis to the whites who colonized America, leaving Indians in a state of poverty and despair. Leave aside for a moment the problems with this analogy, or that from my reading of history, it is the Israelis who are closer to the Indians; they are trying to regain a bit of sovereignty over a portion of their historic homeland to which they and their culture and religion have links of thousands of years, despite being surrounded and greatly outnumbered by hostile "others." Even assuming for the sake of argument that the Palestinian-Indian analogy is correct, who on campus is urging that universities divest from American companies until the U.S. ceases its illegal occupation of Indian lands that were not only the property of Indian nations before whites arrived, but were also "promised" to Indians by hundreds of treaties, nearly all of which have been broken over the last two hundred plus years by the U.S. government?

Take Jews out of the picture, and a different standard applies.

The Problem of Distorting History

A large part of the current anti-Israel campaign is based on historical distortion. This is the stock-in-trade of Holocaust deniers, sophisticated white supremacists, and some black supremacists, too. They disfigure history by omitting a fact here, a fact there, then turning the "story" on its head, knowing that most people are ill-prepared to find where the error is.

It is one thing to have different interpretations of historical events—one would hardly expect a Palestinian child in Gaza and a Jewish child in Tel Aviv to view the history of the Middle East from the same vantage point. But basic facts are just that.

Anti-Israel activists on campus are increasingly trying to paint Israel as the functional equivalent of apartheid-era South Africa. Israel, it is claimed, is a country where only Jews have rights, where those in control are whites who came to "colonize" indigenous people who were viewed as inferior, just as in South Africa.

But to make this case requires historical distortion that wipes out the connection between Jews and the land of Israel even more completely than the most fervent white supremacist would want to vaporize the rightful place of people of color in America. Indeed, to paint this picture requires not only denying the history of the Jewish people, but also distorting the Jewish religion.

Whereas whites had no history in South Africa before they came to colonize it, Jews—who come in all races (including blacks from Ethiopia)—have had a deep and long connection with the land of Israel. . . .

Jews lived in Israel in ancient times, and continued to live there throughout the ages. Jewish sovereignty was lost to invading armies—the Babylonians and later the Romans—but to the Jews dispersed around the world, the land remained the focus. When Jews began their Babylonian exile, Psalm 137 expressed the centrality of their homeland to their identity: "If I forget thee, O Jerusalem, let my right hand forget her cunning." That psalm begins: "By the rivers of Babylon, there we sat down, yes, we wept, when we remembered Zion."

How much of this history and liturgy is ever mentioned by those who want to describe Israel as a "settler-colonialist" state? Their story usually begins with the persecution of European Jews in the nineteenth century and their return to their homeland in the twentieth century. While it is hard to imagine that anyone of goodwill would question the need for a state where Jews can provide for their own self-defense, especially after the Holocaust, the legitimacy of the State of Israel is not based on what the Nazis did. Rather, it is based on the historic connection and continual presence of Jews in the land of Israel.

This is not to say that there is not an Arab history in the region too. There is, of course. Some might point out that there was never an Arab government over "Palestine," only a Jewish one before the Roman, Turkish, and English occupations. Some might point to the Palestinian national identity as a recently minted reaction to the organized presence of Jews. (Beforehand there had been instead a pan-Arab identity; in fact, before 1948 the word "Palestinian" connoted not an Arab, but a Jew living in the land of Israel.) Regardless, there is a Palestinian national identity now that requires respect for its right to self-determination. But just as Palestinians have the right to self-determination, so do Jews. Those who assert that Israel doesn't have a right to exist—anti-Zionists—are denying to Jews alone the rights claimed and respected by every other national group on the globe.

Twisting the Facts

The attempt to paint Israel as a "colonial settler state" like apartheid-era South Africa also distorts contemporary history. Too many people think the story is: There was an Arab state called Palestine, European Jews came and occupied their land, and they won't give it back.

Aside from the fact that there was never an Arab state called Palestine, the Jews who lived in the land, or who came to it in the last century, never desired to rule over another people. The Balfour Declaration of 1917 promised Jews a national homeland in their historic land in Palestine, while insuring the rights of non-Jews in the region. Five years later 80 percent of the land mass of British Mandatory Palestine was removed, and the Arab country of Transjordan (now Jordan) was created.

Territory can be divided; but defining your "enemy" as a devil, which is what is regularly preached to the Palestinians, means there can be no compromise, only violence.

In 1947 the United Nations divided the remaining 20 percent of the British Mandate into two states: one Jewish, one Arab. The Jews accepted the UN's vote. The Arabs declared war, proclaiming they would "drive the Jews into the sea."

The Arab armies tried, but failed, against the Jews, many of whom had just come out of the DP (displaced person) camps of World War II. Israel survived that war and others thrust upon it by its Arab neighbors.

Between 1948 and 1967 Jordan controlled the West Bank, and Egypt ran Gaza. The Arab refugees from the 1948 war roughly equaled the number of Jews from Arab lands who were forced to flee their historic homes. While Israel absorbed these Jews from the Middle East and North Africa (who, now with their descendents, make up nearly half of Israel's Jewish population), the Arab countries kept generation after generation of Arabs as refugees, many in camps.

Where were the calls during these 19 years—either from inside or outside these lands—for an end to "occupation" or the creation of an independent Palestinian state? As long as Arabs ruled and oppressed other Arabs it seems, there was no serious complaint (just as today there is near silence about the Syrian occupation of Lebanon).

The Palestine Liberation Organization (PLO) was created in 1964. That was three years *before* the 1967 war, when the Arab countries would promise yet again to destroy Israel, but Israel would not only survive but also capture the West Bank from Jordan, Gaza from Egypt, and the Golan Heights from Syria. But in 1964 the PLO's covenant, rather than focusing on how to "liberate" the West Bank and Gaza from its Arab brothers, instead called for the total destruction of Israel (within its pre-1967 borders) as an occupier of Arab lands.

Regardless of whether one views Israel's control of the West Bank and Gaza since the 1967 war as legitimate, the fact is that during the Camp David negotiations in the summer of 2000 the Israeli government was willing to agree to a Palestinian state in more than 95 percent of the West Bank and Gaza (including parts of Jerusalem). And rather than offer a counterproposal, the Palestinian leadership walked away from the table and chose to turn the conflict from a territorial one into an existential one. Territory can be divided; but defining your

23

"enemy" as a devil, which is what is regularly preached to the Palestinians, means there can be no compromise, only violence.

Of course, this fact is inconvenient to those who want to paint Israel as apartheid-era South Africa. South Africa didn't want to end its control over the black majority. Israel, on the other hand, wants the Palestinians to be able to set up the infrastructure for their own democratic government. . . .

To say that Jews alone don't have a right to self-determination in a part of their historic homeland is clearly anti-Semitic.

Euphemisms Can't Hide Racism

How many times have you heard "I'm not anti-Semitic, I'm just anti-Zionist?" But to be anti-Zionist is, by definition, to be anti-Semitic.

Zionism is nothing more than a belief that Israel has the right to exist as a homeland for Jews. It says nothing about the policies or programs of the state, merely that it has a right to exist. There are left-wing Zionists and right-wing Zionists—and many in between. Some Zionists are harsh critics of Israeli policies; others are supportive. But the term "Zionist" connotes nothing more than the right of Israel to exist; anti-Zionist means that Israel, regardless of its leaders, policies, or other aspects of how its society is run, has no right to exist.

To say that Jews alone don't have a right to self-determination in a part of their historic homeland is clearly anti-Semitic, despite the effort to hide the bigotry behind a supposed political term.

Likewise, the nonsensical attempt to say that Arabs can't be anti-Semitic, no matter what they say, because they, like Jews, are "Semites." (The word, of course, has always been used to mean prejudice against Jews since it was coined by

Wilhelm Marr in Germany in 1873; the term "Semitic" applies to languages, not people. When was the last time you heard an Arab group complain about "anti-Semitism" when Arabs were discriminated against?)

It is a sign of bigotry when people try to use code words to "explain" away their defamation of a group. Whites opposed to the civil rights movement knew it was "politically incorrect" to say they were anti-black, so they used code words such as "anti-busing." Right-wing anti-Semites who want to maintain the fiction that they are not bigoted use code words such as "international bankers" to defame Jews. The word "anti-Zionist" is of the same mold in the lexicon of the left, and it should fool no one. Anti-Zionism is anti-Semitism.

Further evidence of this anti-Semitism is the penchant among self-proclaimed anti-Zionists to take language associated with the Holocaust and twist it around to label Israelis as Nazis and Israeli leaders as [Adolf] Hitler. No unbiased person could use terminology associated with the mass murder of nearly six million Jews and countless others (including Communists, gays, anti-Nazis, Roma, and Jehovah's Witnesses), many in purposely-built execution chambers, and suggest that the Israelis were engaged in a similar enterprise. And even if some anti-Zionists refuse to recognize either the history or the complexities of the conflict, why do they use the "Nazi" nomenclature to complain only about Israel? Why not use it to describe Rwanda, for example?

The answer is simple: Jews are in the equation, so a different standard applies. Likewise no one on the left would have the temerity to claim that the worst excesses of corporate America are comparable to the horrors of the Middle Passage. Such a comparison would be understood to be both gross overstatement and an immoral diminishing of the terror of genocide—especially so if a targeted corporation were run by an African American. So why the almost gleeful comparison of Israelis to Nazis? Don't know? See Bigotry 101.

A Compromise of Principles

Forget about Israel for a moment. Look at the forces that "progressive" anti-Israel groups are supporting, if not affirmatively, at least by their silence in the face of suicide bombings and other acts of terror: the Palestinian Authority [PA], which is universally understood to be thoroughly corrupt, Islamic Jihad, Hamas, Hizballah.

None of these groups can be said to have a "progressive" agenda. Some are functionally fascist. Are they models of, say, women's rights? Gay rights? Respect for diversity? Models of concern for workers' rights?

Hamas, Hizballah, and Islamic Jihad, in particular, have visions of society that are not that much different than that of the Taliban.

The left has prided itself as a champion of the rights of racial, religious, ethnic, and sexual minorities. But it is willing to support groups that overtly oppress people in exactly these ways because they oppose (and commit acts of violence against) an organized Jewish presence on one-sixth of one percent of the land in the "Arab world."

It takes a great deal of prejudice to overlook basic principles in order to provide enthusiastic support for groups whose main "asset" is hatred of an "enemy." The left's abandonment of its principles in its reflexive support for these fascistic anti-Israel terror groups is very troubling. It says that hatred of Israel is stronger than the left's core human values.

Go back to Bigotry 101. Assume the head of one state—India or Pakistan, for example—offered to pay $25,000 to the families of people in the other country who would go into a crowded area and blow themselves up, taking with them as many of the "other's" civilians as they could. Progressive folk would be outraged, and would call this barbaric and against basic principles of how governments should behave. Further, if the state offering this functional "bounty" for the murder of civilians was at the same time pleading poverty, at least some eyebrows would be raised.

But Iraq's Saddam Hussein has offered such a bounty on Jews in Israel. There has not been a peep of protest from the left, let alone questioning how a country that complains of starvation and disease because of international sanctions for its failure to entertain weapons inspectors has enough money to pay huge bonuses for suicide bombings (separate budget lines, perhaps?).

Why can't progressives take the Israeli experience, put it in an American context, and ask what they think America would do?

Or recall the left's great tradition of protecting children from exploitation, from its focus on American child labor in sweat shops 100 years ago to current efforts to target these same problems in an era of globalization. How can it be that the left speaks out loudly and eloquently if a child is forced to work long hours for low pay anywhere in the world, but remains silent (or even applauds) when a Palestinian child is dressed up as, and told to aspire to be, a suicide bomber who will one day kill him or herself along with Jewish men, women, and children?. . .

Why can progressives not empathize with Israelis who see their children blown up in a pizzeria in Jerusalem, and then find the event celebrated in art at a Palestinian exhibit? Why can progressives not understand that Israelis have every right to be disturbed when they are regularly demonized in sermons in mosques in Gaza and the West Bank and on Arab television in terms directly plagiarized from Nazi propaganda?

Why can't progressives take the Israeli experience, put it in an American context, and ask what they think America would do? What would America do if the Canadian government were the functional equivalent of the PA, and tens of thousands of American civilians (to approximate the relative proportion of Israelis) were being blown up by terrorists harbored and helped by the Canadians? I suspect the American response would be harsher than anything the Israelis have done, that such a response would have the overwhelming support of the American people, and that even if progressives didn't approve of such actions, they would at least understand why those targeted by terrorists had a right to feel concerned.

But apparently when it comes to Jews in Israel, there is no such capacity for empathy and imagination. The Jew, then, becomes a complete "other," unlike the rest of humanity in any way. The capacity to imagine what it is like to be a Palestinian, but not an Israeli, is anti-Semitism.

Examining Ourselves

Bigotry is at its most blinding when a person can see hatred if it comes from someone of a different political persuasion, but can't see the same bigotry coming from within.

The drive to boycott and divest from companies doing business with Israel is being propelled not just by distortions of history, but by turning a blind eye to (or in fact promoting) anti-Semitism.

Progressive groups have been very good at pointing out anti-Semitism from the far right, for example, when hateful tracts such as the forgery *Protocols of the Elders of Zion* or Hitler's *Mein Kampf* are promoted by neo-Nazis, skinheads and other white supremacists.

Yet the same material is being hawked widely in the Arab media. Medieval European anti-Semitic claims—such as that Jews kill non-Jewish kids to use their blood for making Passover matzah—are printed as front-page truthful stories in many Arab newspapers around the world. And at the World Conference Against Racism in Durban [South Africa] in summer 2001, anti-Semitic tracts, including the *Protocols*, were distributed. An Arab lawyers group even printed and prominently displayed enlargements of anti-Semitic cartoons. Anti-Semitic posters and banners were ubiquitous.

But left groups, which would have blasted these same items from hard-right groups, were conspicuously silent. It was almost as if there were a belief that *Mein Kampf* printed in its original German would be anti-Semitic, but an Arab edition not.

To blame Israel for the terrorism of 9/11 would be like blaming blacks for the terrorism of the Ku Klux Klan.

A few days after the Durban conference ended, the attacks of September 11 occurred. And again events were twisted in an anti-Semitic way.

The most egregious fabrications were the charges in many Arab and Islamic countries that Jews were behind the attacks. Polls showed that 48 percent of Pakistanis, for example, believed in such a Jewish conspiracy.

Where were the voices on the left and on the campus pointing to this clear case of bigotry? If mainstream voices in many countries blamed American blacks or gays for the purposeful spreading of AIDS worldwide, you'd expect progressives to expose and protest this hatred. But not when the victims are Jews, apparently.

Could this be because many voices on campus also blame Israel and the Jews for 9/11 (either alone, or in conjunction with "American policies")? Not as secret controllers of the planes or plotters of the crimes, but as morally responsible because of Israeli relations with the Palestinians. Those who make that charge again engage in factual distortion.

The plot to attack the World Trade Center was hatched before the collapse of the peace process, when it looked as if a negotiated settlement between the Israelis and the Palestinians, supported by the United States, was a good bet. The prospect of peace, meaning that Arabs would accept non-

Arabs as permanent sovereign neighbors in the Middle East, is anathema to Islamicists. So, to the extent that Israel may have entered into the mindset of the terrorists, any progress toward a peace settlement between the Palestinians and the Israelis would have *angered* the terrorists, not defused them, because peace would mean that Israel would continue to exist. To blame Israel for the terrorism of 9/11 would be like blaming blacks for the terrorism of the Ku Klux Klan, since in both cases their mere existence was an impetus for the terrorists. But why do campus activists and others on the left who would clearly see the bigotry in the example of blacks in the South not see it when it comes to Jews in Israel?

Terrorism, after all, is in essence a hate crime writ large. Since when it is permissible for the left to "blame the victim" for a hate crime? A woman, no matter how scantily dressed, does not invite rape. Some straight people are made uncomfortable by gays, but would any progressive person tolerate the suggestion that Matthew Shepard was in some way responsible for his own horrid murder? Or that "black crime" might have angered the executioners of James Byrd?

9/11 was a mass murder. There is never any excuse for mass murder, period. But the willingness to bring Jews, Israel, and by extension the American support for Israel into an "explanation" is not only perverse, but bigoted. It is to be expected that a hard-right racist such as [former Klansman] David Duke would make such a claim; but following 9/11, some student groups, including a prominent one at NYU, promoted and distributed Duke's "analysis" as correct.

Promoting a Double Standard

Criticism of Israeli policies is fine if it is made in the same manner as one would criticize the policies of any other country (including Arab countries and the U.S.), and the "remedies" called for are of the same caliber. (In other words, "divestiture" is by definition a tool of bigotry unless it is employed against other countries whose policies are clearly more problematic—by any measure—than Israel's.)

Criticism of Israeli policies is fine if it is proportional and not reflective of a double standard. For example, it would strike educated people as nonsense or worse if a police department spent all its time chasing graffiti "artists" and none of its time going after robbers, rapists, and murderers. Likewise, even if one believes that Israel's human rights record is far from perfect, it is clearly much better than that of the Sudanese, who enslave non-Muslim blacks in the south of the country; the Saudis, who refuse women even the most basic human rights; the Iranians, who suppress the Bahai; the Egyptians, who oppress gays; the Chinese, who repress the Tibetans, etc.

Criticism of Israeli policies is fine if it is not accompanied by a marked increase in anti-Semitic activity. Since the beginning of the movement for divestiture, Jews have been called "kike"; a rock was thrown at a student's window that sported an Israeli flag; a Hillel building's glass door was shattered by a cement block; swastikas were drawn on a sukkah; death threats were shouted at a rally of Jewish students; taunts such as "Hitler didn't finish the job" were yelled; graffiti saying "God Hates Jews" and "Burn the Torah" were painted. If anti-civil rights protestors in the 1960s claimed that their cause wasn't racist, but similar anti-black actions were associated with their movement, progressives wouldn't have been fooled. They mustn't be fooled now.

Go back to Bigotry 101. Jewish students on some campuses are being harassed when they gather collectively, even for events that have nothing to do with the Middle East, such as celebrations of Jewish holidays or commemorations of the Holocaust. If Muslim students had to face protests when they came together to celebrate Islamic holidays, or black students suffered counterdemonstrations on Martin Luther King Day, the left would be quick to see and expose that bigotry.

If progressives want to help the people of the Middle East, they must reject the simplistic lens of bigotry that distorts complex events into all good on one side and all evil on the other. They should rather attempt to find opportunities to help both sides move forward with a progressive agenda. Rather than calling for the boycott of Israeli academics, as some have, American academics should be finding ways to bring their Palestinian and Israeli colleagues together on new, empowering, and imaginative collaborative projects.

Many progressives seem so ensconced in anti-Israel venom that they fail to remember a basic truth they knew well half a century ago: that anti-Semitism is not only the miner's canary (i.e., the early-warning system) of danger to democracy, but also is a highly combustible fuel that propels much of the world's ideological engines of racism and xenophobia, engines that when fully stoked are not only very dangerous, but also difficult to control.

Finally, history is full of examples of times the left in general, and campus progressives in particular, have played an important role in making the world a better, fairer, and more just place. But they cannot do so today if they fail first to confront and reject the anti-Semitism within. This is a defining test for the left. If it is to be a constructive force and promote the conditions for a stable and just peace in the Middle East, it must build such a program on a foundation that fully rejects the caustic bigotry of anti-Zionism. Unfortunately, so far, it is failing this test miserably.

3

Discrimination Against Christians Is Exaggerated

Tom Krattenmaker

Tom Krattenmaker is a Philadelphia-based writer specializing in religion in public life.

Religious leaders in America claim they face unwarranted hostility from secular liberals in this country. There is some truth to the idea that Christian conservatives are sometimes painted as pushy zealots and the values and morals of society are declining. America, however, is not a battleground between believers and political adversaries, and at a time when many real religious wars are taking place in several countries, Christian conservatives experience too much political and religious freedom to seriously consider themselves victims of persecution.

[T]he] holiday season brought us the "War on Christmas." Now, if we are to believe the promotions for an event starting today in the nation's capital, something bigger and darker is afoot in America: "The War on Christians." . . .

Isn't this more than a bit overblown? And in a time when the country is caught up in a real war with religious overtones, shouldn't the word "war" be tossed around a little less recklessly?

Certainly, liberals and secularists must concede a kernel of truth to the religious conservatives' charges. To the eyes of conservative Christians, much appears to have changed for the worse in American society in recent decades. There are stricter limits on explicitly Christian expression in schools and other public settings. There is growing public acceptance of homosexuality and out-of-wedlock births, while television and movies seem awash with sex, nudity and profanity.

And if the claims of Christian persecution sound shrill, so do those of secular Americans who sometimes equate the political activity of religious conservatives with a crusade to replace our Constitution-based government with a hard-edged theocracy.

A Gross Exaggeration

Still, the rhetoric of persecution . . . rings false. A war on Christians? It sounds more like an exaggerated scare tactic aimed at grabbing attention, rallying the troops and sowing deeper division between the opposing sides in the ongoing debate over the proper role of religion in the public square. Worse, it trivializes the true persecution of Christians in the early history of the church and the real abuse unleashed on Christians today in some corners of the world.

Christians in America are hardly being thrown to the lions. In many ways, the political and social values of conservative Christians are carrying the day. We are in the second term of the most faith-friendly, explicitly Christian presidency in many a decade. Not only has President [George W.] Bush talked a good game with evangelicals, but his administration has backed it with dollars for faith-based initiatives and abstinence-education programs. Hollywood is producing more Christian-friendly movies while Christian news media, Christian music, Christian novels and other forms of Christian pop culture continue making their strong mark on society.

Nevertheless, the rhetoric of persecution and oppression seems irresistible to many. Nowhere was the theme of Christian oppression more vividly on display, and combatively expressed, than at Justice Sunday III, held Jan. 8 [2006] at a predominantly African-American congregation in north Philadelphia on the eve of the Senate hearings on Supreme Court nominee Samuel Alito. . . .

The event, televised nationally on Christian networks, was advertised as a rally against the "tyranny" of a supposedly activist and anti-Christian judiciary. But it wasn't long before [the Rev. Herbert] Lusk and the other speakers were railing against a wider litany of assaults on people of faith: abortion, gay unions, restrictions on public religious expression—full-scale oppression of the church. . . .

"We are facing, like we never have before, this hostility against the people of God," roared Lusk, a former running back for the Philadelphia Eagles and the leader of a church whose community outreach work has received more than $1 million in federal funding from President Bush's faith-based initiatives program. "Don't fool with the church, because the church has buried many a critic, and all the critics that we have not buried, we're making funeral arrangements for them!"

What Real War Looks Like

Sadly, real religious war is being fought, causing real burials. We have war, or something very close to it, between the Shiites and Sunnis in Iraq. And—at least as it's perceived by those waging it—there is the religious war of the Iraqi insurgents who invoke jihad in their deadly attacks on American soldiers and their fellow Iraqis.

While religious conservatives gather in Washington today, another terrifying prospect looms over our country and world that makes the claims of [Rick] Scarborough [leader of Vision America] and his co-religionists appear especially trivial. We could be headed toward an international showdown over the nuclear program of the theocratic Islamic government in Iran. John Bolton, U.S. ambassador to the United Nations, has spoken recently of the need for the United States to use "all the tools at our disposal" to eliminate the threat.

Imagine some of the possibilities should diplomacy fail: U.S. forces facing a religiously motivated enemy as they move in to take out the nuclear installations (or government) in the event airstrikes prove insufficient; American interests in the Middle East and elsewhere threatened by retaliatory attacks. Worse yet, imagine a nuclear weapon in the hands of a militant Muslim government with a contempt for Israel and its staunch "infidel" supporter, the United States. Given the crusader overtones of U.S. foreign policy since 9/11, these scenarios could take on the appearance of a real war on Christians. May they never come to pass.

So, for our domestic debates, let's find a more appropriate, more sober vocabulary. Many words might describe what's going on between conservative Christians and their political opponents today. "War"? That's not one of them.

4

The Government Should Protect Americans from Religious Intrusion

James F. Harris

James F. Harris is a philosophy professor at the College of William and Mary. He has written two books and several articles for both domestic and foreign journals.

Current U.S. government members have a responsibility to honor the separation of church and state principles established by the Founding Fathers. This separation of church and state was created to protect American citizens against a papal system that could force a government-sanctioned religion on people who do not share those beliefs and give the ruling party a claim to divine authority. This separation is not discrimination against religion, but rather insurance against discrimination.

Questions about the proper place of religion in a democracy and the separation of church and state remain in the news. In the United States, legal and social battles about the proper place to draw the line between religion and government are being waged around the issues of abortion, gay marriage, faith-based social services, and other well-publicized flash points of conflict between sacred beliefs and secular authority. And with the political influence of religious conservatives evidenced in the 2004 presidential election, the issue of religious influence on affairs of state is likely to remain a mat-

James F. Harris, "Religion and Liberal Democracy," *Humanist*, vol. 66, May–June 2006. Copyright 2006 by the American Humanist Association. Reproduced by permission of the author.

ter of importance and controversy for the foreseeable future. Thus the secularism and church-state separation of liberal democratic theory are under renewed attack. So reexamining the principles underlying secular government becomes not simply a matter of leisurely philosophical speculation but one of extreme political and practical urgency.

The principle of separation of church and state is essential for providing for and preserving both religious freedom and the long-term continuation of the peaceful stability of a well-ordered, liberal democracy—where human equality and human freedom are regarded as fundamental and intrinsic goods and where more human freedom is recognized as better than less. But leaders of what is commonly called the religious right have been attempting to tear down the Jeffersonian wall of separation between church and state (as did many religionists in [American president] Thomas Jefferson's own day). So it is necessary to clarify what is at stake in this struggle.

Many people don't realize that the phrase "separation of church and state" isn't found anywhere in the Constitution of the United States. The celebrated First Amendment simply places a prohibition on Congress by saying that "Congress shall make no law respecting an establishment of religion, or prohibiting the free exercise thereof." This language severely limits the actions of the federal government but says nothing about limitations on state governments or on religion itself. On the contrary, for many alive at the time of ratification, one intention of the restraint on Congress appears to have been to give state governments free rein in religious matters. It wasn't until 1868, when the Fourteenth Amendment applied the Bill of Rights to the states, that states were constitutionally required to be religiously neutral.

While various Supreme Court decisions have since used the language and imagery of the "wall of separation between church and state," the phrase originated in the famous letter Thomas Jefferson wrote to the Danbury, Connecticut, Baptist

Association during his first term as president in 1802. In this letter he also wrote that "religion is a matter which lies solely between man & his god." This was a principled position: later in his *Autobiography* he made it clear that his thinking included "the Jew and the Gentile, the Christian and the Mahometan, the Hindoo, and infidel of every denomination." Jefferson had the genius to recognize that the fundamental issue of religious freedom extends beyond the simple mutual toleration of different Christian denominations for each other.

Establishing Boundaries

Before examining the importance of the separation of church and state in liberal democratic theory, it is necessary to clarify two important presuppositions of that theory. The first is a certain view of human nature and the second (dependent to some extent on the first) is the distinction between the private lives of citizens and the public arena in which legislation or public policy is proposed, debated, and then either approved or defeated.

Liberal democratic theory is committed to a general philosophic view of human nature that can be traced to the Enlightenment. Are human equality and human freedom intrinsic goods? Is it the role of government to protect and nurture these goods? Does the ultimate source of legitimate political authority lie in the citizens of a republic? Liberal democratic theory answers in the affirmative and views humans as rational beings capable of determining and regulating their own social, economic, and political affairs. The "liberal" aspect of liberal democratic theory takes its meaning from the philosophical rather than the political usage of the term—a meaning that is derived from "liberty." Both [German philosopher] Immanuel Kant and Thomas Jefferson endorsed this view of human nature. Reacting against the dominant Christian theological view that human nature was fundamentally corrupt and in need of divine guidance and deliverance from itself,

Kant and Jefferson endorsed the optimistic view that regarded human beings as fundamentally rational and profoundly educable. Knowledge resulting from free, unfettered inquiry was viewed as providing not only the basis for understanding the natural world but also for humans understanding themselves, including their social and political selves. Thus human beings came to be regarded as embodying the ability to consider and value the common good and to provide for the social and political arrangements that improve the human condition. The notion of self-government had to be proceeded by the belief that human beings are capable of self-government.

Clarifying the distinction between the private lives of the citizens of a democracy and the public arena in which public policy and legislation are debated and formulated is crucial to liberal democratic theory. [English philosopher] John Locke made clear, for example, in *A Letter Concerning Toleration*, that the business of the civil magistrate and the business of the church must be completely distinct. Locke maintained that "the only business of the church is the salvation of souls" and the only circumstances in which the state has an interest are those in which the commonwealth stands to suffer some prejudice or injury.

But if a democratic government is to nurture and maximize human freedom then it must provide constitutional protections for a diversity of beliefs across a wide spectrum—including religious beliefs.

The distinction between public and private life is one Jefferson used as the crux of his justification for his wall separating church and state. Not only is religion a private matter in Jefferson's view, there are also pernicious effects due to the mingling of private matters of religion and public affairs of state. [American president] James Madison concurred, claiming that the papal system, wherein church and the state aren't separated, represents "the worst form of governments." The wall of separation was thus intended to prevent what Thomas Paine later called the "adulterous connection of church and state."

Putting Aside Personal Conviction

At the time the U.S. Constitution was framed there was considerable debate amongst the various states concerning whether government should establish recognized connections between religion (i.e., Protestant Christianity) and the state or whether it should explicitly disestablish such connections. Some delegates, insisting that the United States was a Christian nation, tried but failed in an attempt to include such recognition in the Constitution. Given the pressure from various religious groups and clergy, and given their own deeply held religious beliefs, it is an often-overlooked act of statesmanship of enormous proportion that the delegates to the Constitutional Congress were able to set aside their own particular beliefs in the framing of the document. The de facto separation of church and state created in the Constitution by this absence of references to Christianity or other religions was widely and strongly criticized by many religious leaders at the time. Debates in state legislatures concerning adoption of the Constitution were often heated, with much concern expressed about religious freedom and with several states insisting that a guarantee of religious freedom be included in a bill of rights. This debate led to the First Amendment in 1789. The movement toward complete disestablishment of religion in all of the states was a slow, gradual, multifaceted process that involved Congress, the Office of the President, the Supreme Court, and state legislatures and continued until the mid-twentieth century. Indeed, some might say it still continues today.

But if a democratic government is to nurture and maximize human freedom then it must provide constitutional protections for a diversity of beliefs across a wide spectrum—including religious beliefs. In order to do this, a constitutional democracy needs to provide constitutional guarantees that prohibit civil penalties, denial of civil privileges, or granting of special civil privileges on the basis of religious beliefs (or lack thereof) on the part of any citizen.

Locke's words are still directly on point in this regard: his claim that "it is above all things necessary to distinguish exactly the business of civil government from that of religion" provides a mechanism to put an end to the otherwise endless religious controversies in a pluralistic society that prevent the peaceful and smooth functioning of a well-ordered society. The fundamental claims that are to be incorporated into the constitution must be justifiable to all citizens, and this cannot be done if the justification appeals to one set of religious beliefs rather than another. In order to construct a constitution on principles that all citizens will agree to, one must appeal only to human reason. This is the lesson that is preserved in [American] philosopher John Rawls' principle of political legitimacy (*Political Liberalism*, 1993), which considers such matters as "who has the right to vote, or what religions are to be tolerated, or who is to be assured equality of opportunity, or to hold property."

Debunking the Paradox Myth

However, not everyone agrees that the fundamental constitutional issues should be debated and decided by appeal only to reason. For example, [American philosopher] Nicholas Wolterstorff maintains that the separation of public civic life from private religious life discriminates against religious believers by requiring them to act politically while denying or ignoring their religious beliefs, and that setting their religious beliefs aside in such circumstances might very well be contrary to or a violation of those religious beliefs. This situation generates a paradox for liberal democratic theory, according to Wolterstorff, since liberal democratic theory is based upon the fundamental commitment to equality and freedom; however, for the religious person, such a commitment might be based upon religious belief. In his view, by denying the religious person the right to appeal to religious belief to justify the most fundamental principles of democracy, liberal democratic theory would presumably be denied the support of the religious person, and the religious person would presumably be denied the freedom to act upon his or her religious belief.

To respond to Wolterstorff's criticism of the separation of public civic reason and private religious belief, it is necessary to be clear about exactly what his complaint is. In order to generate the apparent paradox, it appears that Wolterstorff must be claiming that the religious person's commitment to equality and freedom is based solely and exclusively upon religious belief. Ought a person be allowed to appeal to religious belief as the exclusive justification for valuing equality and individual freedom on the constitutional level and would the failure to allow such an appeal be paradoxical to liberal democratic theory? The answers to these questions become apparent when the questions are generalized. . . .

To best ensure that a society is secure, stable, and peacefully well ordered for the long term, a liberal democracy must be protected from the incursion of religion in all forms and on all levels. It doesn't take a religious jihad to threaten a liberal democracy; it only takes allowing the "the first experiment on our liberties," as Madison writes—the first wedge of religion into the structure of the state.

Certainly not all fanatics are religious, but the ones who are tend to operate on the same principle: that some religious belief or claim must be placed in the position of ultimate authority. The religious fanatic who opposes abortion by bombing abortion clinics acts on the same principle as the religious fanatic who burns an embassy in protest of so-called blasphemous cartoons published in the embassy's home country.

Both are resorting to violence to damage the state in order to prompt a change in its laws or policies on the basis of some religious belief. Both are religious fanatics acting upon religious beliefs that are immune to reason. The only difference is in the magnitude of the attacks and the number of victims. Both are religious terrorists to a peaceful, well-ordered liberal democracy.

A Delicate Balance

Among those who at present debate the relationship between church and state, there would undoubtedly be more agreement about the necessity for the separation on the constitutional level than there would be about the necessity for the separation (and the meaning of separation) within a constitutional democracy. Once a democratic constitution is in place, as the long history of conflicts and court decisions in the United States makes clear, fixing the boundaries between religion and the state becomes trickier. On the legislative level, where individual laws and public policies are determined, what is the proper role of religious beliefs? There must be additional restraints operative that establish a prima facie obligation upon citizens to refrain from appealing to privately held religious beliefs in the public forum in which the affairs of state are conducted. The difficulty will be in justifying restraints upon appeals to religious beliefs given the constitutional guarantees of the disestablishment of religion (that is now taken as prohibiting any governmental endorsement of religion) and the free exercise of religion (that is now taken as prohibiting any governmental interference with religion).

According to Robert Audi in his book *Religious Commitment and Secular Reason*, a citizen in a liberal democracy has a prima facie obligation to appeal only to secular reason or to be sufficiently motivated only by secular reason to support or oppose legislation or policy in the public arena. If a person is originally motivated solely by religious belief or has a religious belief as the sole reason for advocating or opposing a particular action by the state, then that belief or that reason needs to be reformulated into a rationale or an argument that appeals to human reason.

Perhaps the most significant feature of religious reason, and perhaps the feature from which all the other differences between religious reason and secular reason derive, is the oft-touted claim by believers that religious reasons carry an infallible supreme authority that guarantees the truth of such claims against all potential epistemic defeaters. However, allowing appeals to such religious reasons, held to be infallible, in the public arena where laws and public policies are made, would result in what Audi calls a "clash of Gods" and a "battle to the death," that is, an epistemic dead end from which there is no retreat or escape. This would obviously threaten the peaceful and well-ordered stability of a liberal democracy.

Extending the free exercise of religion to the public arena threatens to destroy the underlying theoretical framework of the very democratic guarantee of the free exercise of religion itself.

But, is not disagreement and conflict simply one of the prices to be paid for a liberal democracy? There are numerous cases where the free exercise of religion and privately held religious beliefs have apparently come into conflict with public reason. The followers of Christian Science, for example, often refuse conventional medical treatment for their minor children on the basis of religious beliefs. Some fundamentalist Muslim parents force female circumcision upon their minor daughters on the basis of religious beliefs. Gay marriage and abortion are opposed by many on the basis of religious beliefs. And some support the public display of the Ten Commandments on government property on the basis of religious beliefs.

Separation Ensures Freedom

In each of these cases, the proper approach is to separate the religious interest from the civic interest and to require, in those cases where the religious interest is said to overlap with the civic interest, that the matter of civic concern be put in nonreligious terms. Most importantly, in a pluralistic, liberal democracy this must be done in a way that guarantees equal protection, in this case religious parity, for all.

How might equilibrium amongst competing religious beliefs and equal protection ever be achieved unless a wall of separation between church and state is maintained? The simple, straightforward answer is that it cannot. Equal treatment and the establishment of religion are inversely proportional. To the extent that one religion is given preferential or privileged treatment, others are denied equal treatment.

Locke maintained that citizens should be allowed free exercise of religion except in cases where such exercise harms society or poses the possibility of social harm. It is certainly permissible for people to believe whatever they prefer on whatever grounds they choose in their private lives. However, if those same beliefs are used as the basis for legislation or public policy, it is easy to see that a line has been crossed where the introduction of private religious beliefs into the public forum becomes damaging to society. Extending the free exercise of religion to the public arena threatens to destroy the underlying theoretical framework of the very democratic guarantee of the free exercise of religion itself. In a liberal democracy the exclusion of religion from the government arena is the only way to provide for the peaceful stability of a well-ordered society that protects the free expression of religion in the private lives of citizens.

5

The Government Should Allow Religion in Education

Noah Feldman

Noah Feldman is a professor at New York University's School of Law and a fellow of the New America Foundation. He is also the author of Divided by God: America's Church-State Problem—and What We Should Do About It.

Those who argue that religion has no place in public because church and state should be separate and those who declare that separation of church and state violates the First Amendment are misinterpreting the Constitution and the intention of its framers. The solution to this controversy is to eliminate the problems caused by money and coercion. By allowing religion a public place in society but refusing to fund strictly religious groups and activities with government funds, this debate could be resolved.

Michael Newdow, a California atheist, has gained plenty of notoriety [since] he got a case all the way to the U.S. Supreme Court contending that children in general—his daughter in particular—must not recite the words "under God" in the Pledge of Allegiance in school. Why not? Because he believes the words, which were added in 1954, violate the separation of church and state.

You may have thought Newdow had gone away. After all, the high court threw out the case because he doesn't have custody of his daughter. But he's back, making the challenge again on behalf of the parents of other children. A lower federal court has already ruled in his favor.

Noah Feldman, "God, Government, and You," *USA Today*, October 17, 2005, p. 15A. Copyright © 2005, USA Today. Reproduced by permission of the author.

Newdow is once again raising hackles and crystallizing just how much a quintessential question—one the Framers of the Constitution thought they had nailed—has returned to tear at the very definition of what it is to be an American. It's a question that's more divisive today than partisan politics or even religious beliefs: How much of a role should religion play in public life?

The Divide

The country is split between two camps. On one side are those who, like Newdow, think that government should be secular, and that the laws should make it so. On the other are those who believe that common values derived from religion should inform our public decisions just as they inform our private lives. An extreme example is former Alabama judge Roy Moore, who put up a 2[frac12]-ton granite monument to the Ten Commandments in the state Supreme Court building and refused to take it down, even when the federal courts ordered him to.

The two sides fight it out on a very basic level in debates about when life begins—the issue in the abortion and stem cell research debates. And when it ends—the issue that engulfed the nation in the Terri Schiavo case. Tell me whether you think religion should play a role in government decisions, and I'll tell you where you come out on these core debates.

Even the ever-controversial debate over same-sex marriage is really about religion and government. Opponents of same-sex marriage say that marriage has a traditional religious meaning as the union of one man and one woman. They don't want the government to change that. Supporters say that the religious definition of marriage has no bearing on the purely legal question of whether everyone should have equal access to a benefit given by the government.

These hard questions, which reach the U.S. Supreme Court so often, are lightning rods for debate because they go to the very heart of who we are as a nation.

Is there an answer?

Actually, the Framers had a pretty good one, not that either side is reading their intent right. Both like to claim that the Constitution is on their side and want to enlist the Founding Fathers for their preferred position.

If we were serious about getting back to the Framers' way of doing things, we would adopt their two principles: no money and no coercion.

The Newdow-leaners, or "legal secularists," point out that God is conspicuously absent from the Constitution, and that the First Amendment prohibits an establishment of religion even as it guarantees "the free exercise thereof." They conclude that religion and government must be separated by a high protective wall. The Moore sympathizers, or "values evangelicals," counter that the words "separation of church and state" also do not appear in our founding document. Reminding us that the Founders' America was almost entirely Christian— and 95% Protestant—they conclude that Judeo-Christian values are the true basis for our national project.

Compromise Is the Solution

Both sides are only half right. The Framers believed to a man in the importance of the liberty of conscience, and they barred a national established religion in order to protect that value. Obsessed with taxes, they thought that an official religion would infringe on religious liberty by spending tax dollars for religious purposes. They also knew they could never agree on a national religion, given their own diverse denominations. But so long as no money was involved and the government was not coercing anyone in religious affairs, they had no great objection to religious symbols in the public sphere. Thomas Jefferson excepted, all the early presidents declared public days of Thanksgiving and prayer—even James Madison, author of the First Amendment.

If we were serious about getting back to the Framers' way of doing things, we would adopt their two principles: no money and no coercion. This compromise would allow plenty of public religious symbolism, but it would also put an end to vouchers for religious schools. God could stay in the Pledge, but the faith-based initiative would be over, and state funds could reach religious charities only if they were separately incorporated to provide secular social services.

The public could logically embrace this modest proposal, and the zealots on both sides should think it over. Secularists want all Americans to feel included as citizens, but right now, many evangelicals feel excluded by the limits on their religious expression. Meanwhile, values evangelicals should recognize that state funding of religion means their own tax dollars are going to support radical religious teachings that they abhor.

Our nation today is more religiously diverse than ever. No longer Judeo-Christian (if we ever were), we are now Judeo-Christian-Muslim-Buddhist-Hindu-agnostic-atheist. That means we need a new church-state solution to reconcile our religious differences with our common faith in America. The Framers' own views can lead the way—and we should follow.

6

Religious Expression Is Discouraged by the U.S. Military

Angelo M. Codevilla

Angelo M. Codevilla is a professor at Boston University, a Claremont Institute fellow, and a senior editor of American Spectator.

According to the U.S. government, God cannot be a copilot to members of the U.S. armed forces. An organization that asks its members to risk its lives has no business asking them to risk their faith as well. Restricting chaplains from practicing their beliefs, giving spiritual direction to soldiers, and pretending as though religion is of no importance ostracizes those who are serious about their faith. Guidelines that promote an indifference to God in order to appease a secular minority will only deter religious individuals, who constitute most of the armed forces, from military service.

Arguably the worst, most gratuitous, most ominous act inflicted on America in living memory was Secretary of Defense Donald Rumsfeld's August 29, 2005 promulgation of guidelines for religious expression in the U.S. Air Force—intended as a model for the rest of the armed forces. Their essence is to forbid anyone in uniform from giving "the reasonable perception that [the Armed Forces, and hence the U.S. government] support any religion over other religions or the

Angelo M. Codevilla, "The Atheist Foxhole," *American Spectator*, vol. 39, February 2006. Copyright © The American Spectator 2006. Reproduced by permission.

idea of religion over the choice of no religious affiliation." However, they place no restriction on anyone who might advocate atheism, or mock, or restrict, or cause discomfort to, the religiously observant in any setting. Indeed they are all about placing the U.S. government's weight against talking about the presence, or praying for the guidance or protection, of God. Meanwhile, the Air Force and other services require their members to take instruction in "sensitive" thought and behavior amounting to a secular religion.

Marginalizing religion among people likely to be shot at is always a bad idea. But discouraging religion in forces once headed by George Washington, whose current members come from the most devout sectors of the modern world's most devout country, at the behest of people scarcely present in those forces, shows incompetence more than evil. [Joseph] Stalin's rules for the Red Army in World War II were more God-friendly than Rumsfeld's.

Until recently, traditions and the habits of servicemen combined with common sense to exempt the Armed Forces from the U.S. government's longstanding Kulturkampf [the Roman Catholic policies ruling Germany from 1871 to 1878, enacted by Chancellor Otto von Bismarck] against religion in America. Anyone going up to the Secretary of the Air Force's Pentagon office would pass by a huge mural of an Air Force family going to church, with the words, "Here I am Lord, send me." Cadets at the Naval Academy still pray collectively before common meals. Young men away from home for the first time—at least those who do not simply drink and whore—find religious practice a lifeline that keeps them connected to normal human life. The advent of the "All Volunteer Force" in the 1970s increased the proportion of practicing Christians among both officers and enlisted. Since 9/11, the "foxhole factor" has come into play: The number of atheists is inversely proportional to that of bullets flying. In short, there have been the very opposite of popular pressures for secularization.

Restrictions on Prayer Are Wrong

The excuse that the most recent restrictions on religion are being forced by the courts is insincere. Yes, one Mikey Weinstein filed a suit alleging that the longstanding patterns of behavior at the Air Force Academy amounted to "severe, systemic and pervasive" religious discrimination. But no ruling of the Supreme Court has invalidated them. Nor has any law done so. Yet a few officers wanted to have less Christianity there, and key officials in the Rumsfeld Pentagon agreed. Nor does the excuse wash that the restrictions are necessary for the maintenance of good military order. The pragmatic way to ensure unit cohesion is surely not to displease the many for the sake of the few.

The guidelines are more radical than they seem. "Public prayer," they direct, "should not normally be included"—read, is banned—except in "extraordinary circumstances." The only ones they cite are "mass casualties, preparation for imminent combat, and natural disasters". In essence, the Bush Pentagon lets the name of God be invoked only when absolutely necessary to provide the equivalent of a shot of booze, or of a mood-altering drug. Practically, it treats religion as [German political philosopher Karl] Marx described it: "the opiate of the masses." Prima faciae, even opening a routine meeting with the Pledge of Allegiance flouts the guidelines, because it affirms that America is anything but indifferent to God.

Worse, the guidelines also permit prayer where, "consistent with longstanding military tradition," there are "change of command, promotion ceremonies, or significant celebrations. . ."—but only if such "prayer" is emptied of "specific beliefs" and intended "to add a heightened sense of seriousness or solemnity." How patent unseriousness may add seriousness is part of the Bush White House's closely guarded formula for success. It may not have realized that it outdid the judges who had tried to outlaw the Pledge of Allegiance.

Problems for Chaplains

The guidelines place special restrictions and responsibilities on chaplains. Heretofore they had been allowed, even encouraged, to shepherd men of their own denomination, urge members of other denominations to be faithful to them, and to try to bring the godless to God. Now they are to help restrict their flock's own urges to proselytize, to restrict their own and their flock's religious practices to the guidelines, and above all to give no one the impression that God exists and that it matters. To chaplains who wear the uniform, these are orders. But these orders raise the most fundamental questions of all: What is the chaplain doing in uniform? For whom is he working? To what end?

It is inherently difficult to believe that one is serving God by working in an organization that will penalize you for speaking his name.

A chaplain's job has always been inherently problematic. On the one hand he must do nothing to impair his flock's ability to do their military jobs. On the other, he cannot simply be yet another voice urging people to do what they're told regardless of what they might think. His authority comes from God, on whose behalf he cares for the things that are most important to each individual. For Christian chaplains, Jesus' words "render unto Caesar the things that are Caesar's and unto God the things that are God's" have offered a practical solution to this conflict. In America, a nation explicitly "under God," the chaplains could counsel people to follow the faith's dictates fully, while obeying orders wholeheartedly because the two did not conflict.

But what can a Christian chaplain under the guidelines say when he reads, or someone asks him about, the Gospel's charge to "go out among all nations, baptizing them in the name of the father. . ."? Or what can a Jewish one say when several of his flock are disciplined for gathering together in prayer at the times prescribed by the Law? The free exercise of religion involves speaking and acting in public. Clergymen's stock in trade must be to urge religious practice in everyday life. What can they say, what can serious Christians or Jews think, about an organization in which they risk their lives while demanding that they behave in ways that they believe endanger their immortal souls? It becomes difficult for them to say, I belong here.

It is inherently difficult to believe that one is serving God by working in an organization that will penalize you for speaking his name. But does not one serve God by serving His America? Not if America insists that those who love God shut up about it while those who mock him may do so at will. Whose America is it anyway? It cannot belong equally to people whose views of it are incompatible with one another. The Air Force cadets who charged that a critical mass of evangelicals at the Academy had created an environment they could not stand, and the captain featured in the *New York Times* article that supported them, had every right to tell themselves and the world something like "this isn't me, and this is not my idea of America." And, because their views of America coincided with those of powerful people in Washington, the Bush administration promulgated guidelines congenial to them. But, by the very same token, these guidelines frame an environment unacceptable to serious Christians and Jews.

The all volunteer force lives by attracting people. Its character, and its size, depend on who finds military service attractive. There may exist a pool of young people big enough to fill America's military who combine appetite for physical challenges, tolerance for danger, a spirit of self-sacrifice, discipline, and patriotism, but who don't really care whether America is "under God" or not, who get along just fine without the Ten Commandments, are more bothered by piety than by homosexuality, and are inspired by "sensitivity" training. And perhaps the social changes forced upon the U.S. military in recent years will bring such people out of the woodwork and into uniform. Maybe America will end up with atheist foxholes. But surely these changes tell the families who now actually fill the Armed Forces that maybe the kinds of people who are making the rules should also be doing the fighting.

7

Religious Expression Is Not Discouraged by the U.S. Military

Wayne Adkins

Wayne Adkins is a first lieutenant in the Ohio National Guard. He served in Iraq and as the Task Force Buckeye Public Affairs Officer during Hurricane Katrina relief efforts. Adkins currently serves as executive officer of the 196[th]Mobile Public Affairs Detachment.

Although the military goes to great lengths to accommodate soldiers of every religion, it refuses to acknowledge atheism as a valid belief system. Soldiers cannot list "atheist" as their religious preference on their dog tags and are often forced to perform work details if they choose not to attend religious services. Chaplains should not be permitted to openly mock atheists as chaplains are not allowed to publicly disparage one religion over another. Atheists are no less qualified soldiers than those who believe in God and should be treated with equal respect.

The United States military has gone to great lengths to accommodate soldiers from a variety of religious backgrounds. They provide dietary alternatives, a variety of chaplains and printed materials from every major religion. They have gone as far as accommodating Wiccan rituals and allowing open Satan worship on military bases and ships. But there is one group of soldiers that the military has turned its back on.

Wayne Adkins, "Religious Discrimination Continues in the Military," *American Chronicle*, December 17, 2005. Reproduced by permission.

Atheists are still openly disparaged by chaplains in today's military. Chaplains continue to perpetuate the myth that there are no atheists in foxholes despite the fact that atheists are serving honorably right now in Iraq, Afghanistan and elsewhere. The military's response has been to simply ignore it.

Some chaplains, like Captain Scott McCammon and Major Eric Albertson, have gone as far as saying that atheists are less qualified as soldiers than their religious counterparts. McCammon said in an interview "You can know how to dig a foxhole, but unless you are spiritually fit, you won't have the courage to stick your head out of the hole. I remind them of the old saying, 'There are no atheists in foxholes,' and encourage them not to wait until they get into one to start praying." Albertson has said "commanders recognize that spiritually fit soldiers are better fighters, and can bring a spirit of determination to the mission that is courageous and heroic". . . .

Atheists Deserve Equal Respect

What happens to chaplains who disparage atheist soldiers during interviews with the media? Nothing happens despite the complaints of atheist soldiers. Imagine what would happen if a chaplain said "Jewish soldiers really do believe in the divinity of Jesus when the enemy attacks." The military wouldn't wait for Jewish soldiers to complain. They would reprimand that chaplain quickly and publicly. The implication is exactly the same; that they really believe the same truth that "the rest of us" believe and as soon as they get good and scared they will admit it.

The overt discrimination doesn't end there. Atheists are not allowed to put atheist on their ID tags as a religious preference. Soldiers must put "no preference" or pay to have their own ID tags made if they want them to say atheist. There is a world of difference between having no religious preference and being an atheist. Often soldiers must choose between religious services and work details. Twice in my career I was told to either go to church or pick up trash. Soldiers are often captive audiences for chaplains as well. The first thing that happened when my plane landed after returning from Iraq was a chaplain boarded and held a ten minute devotional on the PA system before soldiers had an opportunity to get off the plane.

Chaplains are allowed to be dogmatic in their sermons. They can state their beliefs from the pulpit even if they contradict other soldiers' beliefs. They wouldn't be able to do their job if they couldn't do that. But when chaplains are speaking to the press and representing the military as an officer, they have absolutely no business singling out a particular group of soldiers and disparaging them because of their beliefs. That is pure and simple bigotry and apparently the senior leadership in the military condones it as they continue to do nothing about it. It's an easy fix. Unlike other religious groups, atheists need no special accommodation. We don't need time for services. We don't need religious literature paid for by taxpayers. We don't need dietary accommodations. We would just like the military to stop denying that we serve and stop disparaging us in the press.

I'll stand shoulder to shoulder with any other American and fight for their religious freedom. I'll also stand toe to toe with any American and fight for my own. Enough is enough.

8

Feminism Discriminates Against Islamic Women in America

Yvonne Yazbeck Haddad, Jane Smith, and Kathleen Moore

Yvonne Yazbeck Haddad is a professor of the history of Islam and Christian-Muslim relations at Georgetown University. Jane Smith is co-director of the Duncan Black Macdonald Center for Christian-Muslim Relations and a professor of Islamic studies at Hartford Theological Seminary. Kathleen Moore is an associate professor of law and society at the University of California–Santa Barbara.

Islamic women in America frequently face discrimination because of their traditional clothing and their beliefs about women's responsibilities. American feminists operate under a set of misconceptions perpetuated in the media that Islamic women are subsequent objects of men's desires, or terrorist, while none of these stereotypes accurately portrays the majority of Islamic women living in the United States.

Muslim Women in the Crucible

Maysa Mounla-Sakkal was elated when she was notified in July of 1994 that she was accepted into Western Reserve's Pediatric Residency Training Program in Cleveland, Ohio. With a medical degree from Aleppo University, she had spent nine years as a medical researcher and nurse in her husband's practice in Syria. As she went through her monthly rotations at Western Reserve, physicians on the teaching staff of the pediatric department completed evaluations of her performance. At the end of her first year, Dr. Mounla-Sakkal's residency was not renewed. She brought a lawsuit against the pediatric department alleging religious and national origin discrimination, harassment, and retaliation. Her suit was dismissed before trial because of a lack of direct evidence, although her deposition shows that before she was hired the teaching staff had made comments about her Arab origin and wanted to know her position with respect to the Arab-Israeli conflict. A female physician on the teaching staff told Mounla-Sakkal that if she wanted to continue to second-year residency, she could not pray in public and would have to take off her headscarf, adding that "babies are afraid" of the headscarf. The attending physician allegedly commented to other clinicians that Muslims ride camels and are backward thinking, that Muslim women walk behind their husbands, and that Islam is inferior to Christianity. Although the incidents that Mounla-Sakkal could point to were clearly inappropriate, under the law they were considered neither frequent nor harsh enough over the course of one year to constitute harassment.

How is a society that is based on the principles of tolerance and egalitarianism supposed to accommodate the demands of an increasingly heterogeneous public? In the United States this question lies at the heart of multicultural accommodation of religious and ethnic minorities. There has been a growing trend toward the acceptance of myriad cultural practices and identities as legitimate forms of self-expression. But at some critical points of intersection between "mainstream" society and its component parts, important trade-offs ensue. For instance, while tolerance of difference is a valued concept, so is the equality of women. When the precepts of a so-called "foreign" belief system appear to offend mainstream perceptions of the equal rights of women, which is to hold sway? According to contemporary American legal standards, the civil rights of women by and large trump the civil liberties of religious or cultural minorities whose inherited traditions, perhaps incidentally, result in sexist or discriminatory treatment.

Legal Complications

Tensions between Islamic traditions and practices and American concepts of women's rights continue to be engaged, argued about, harmonized, negotiated, and renegotiated in varying ways. Unfortunately, prevalent in this dialogue are views that tend to be reductionist—ones that discredit Islam as a peculiarly sexist religion, or Western feminism as a hazardously ideological movement that pits women against men. Such attitudes have not been particularly helpful in working through the controversies that in fact reflect the complex nature of both Islamic and Western societies. These contests are apparent nowhere more than in American courts of law. As Muslims become more confident and assertive of their rights as members of a religious minority in American society, a struggle to balance the sometimes clashing requirements of religious law and secular law ensues. Besides inevitable conflicts that arise between Muslims and non-Muslims—such as Dr. Mounla-Sakkal's complaint against her employers— American courts of law are also more frequently drawn into disputes among Muslims, often on issues of Islamic family law. Some Muslims are pressing American courts to apply Islamic legal rules in instances of family law, making the resolution of disputes arising from the realities of Muslim life in the United States an important although complex part of the American legal terrain.

For many Muslims, the stipulations and directives redacted from the Qur'an and Sunnah [Islamic religious doctrine] still prevail in many Muslim countries, particularly in relation to matters of personal status law and marriage (which in Islam is contractual, not sacramental), treatment of women within the family, divorce, and maintenance of children. While Muslim family law is one of the main targets for Islamic reform in many countries of the world today, for many practicing Muslims in the West it is accepted as the essential core of what makes a society Islamic.

Fiqh, jurisprudence, is very important to observant American Muslims trying to understand what regulations genuinely apply to persons living in non-Muslim majority countries. The implementation of Islamic law in everyday circumstances actually becomes more important in a non-Muslim environment, where it is easy to slip into Western ways without societal constraints based on Qur'anic injunctions. With no school of law predominant in the United States, and with traditional Islamic notions of family relations often at odds with prevailing American ideologies and practices, Muslim leaders are spending considerable time and attention in helping their constituencies understand what is right, appropriate, legal, or not legal in the American context. . . .

Women in hijab *(loose clothing and headscarf) are targets of strong anti-Muslim feeling ranging from hate crimes and violence to discrimination in employment and education.*

The experiences of Muslim women in American courts have been highly productive. In their work on gender, power, and identity among evangelical Christian and Muslim women in the United States, sociologists John Bartkowski and Jen'nan Ghazal Read point out that religion has provided unique cultural repertoires which enable women to affirm their religious values while refashioning their convictions to fit their post-traditional lifestyles. We would add that the law—whether sacred or secular—also helps women to negotiate their place in American society. They are able to stay current and engaged with broader social trends (such as prevailing gender norms) while simultaneously tailoring their own religious identity.

An Increase in Acts of Discrimination

The problem of anti-Muslim discrimination, complicated as it is by the historical relationship between Muslim societies and the West, has become especially pronounced in the United States since the September 11 attacks. The FBI, along with local law enforcement agencies, has reported a huge increase in harassment of Muslims and Arabs, as well as violent crime against their persons and their property. In monitoring workplace discrimination, the Equal Employment Opportunity Commission (the EEOC) has documented hundreds of complaints annually since 9/11 from individuals who allege backlash discrimination because they are—or are perceived to be—Muslim, Arab, Middle Eastern, South Asian, or Sikh. Homes, businesses, and places of worship have been firebombed or vandalized. Individuals have been attacked with guns, knives, fists, incendiary devices, and words.

Many of these cases involve women, most commonly their wearing of a head covering. Women in *hijab* (loose clothing and headscarf) are targets of strong anti-Muslim feeling ranging from hate crimes and violence to discrimination in employment and education. Women wearing headscarves have been spat upon, shoved, and beaten. School children have been harassed by their teachers and classmates and by the parents of other children. The following cases illustrate some of the ways in which this discrimination has been demonstrated, some of them recording incidents that took place even before the 2001 attacks.

On September 30, 2002, the EEOC sued Alamo Rent-a-Car Company because a customer service representative in its Phoenix office, Ms. Bilan Nur, was denied permission to cover her head with a scarf during the Muslim holy month of Ramadan. Alamo had granted Ms. Nur permission to cover during Ramadan in 1999 and 2000, but in December 2001—just three months after the terrorist attacks—the rental company refused to allow her to observe her religious beliefs in relation to dress. Alamo subsequently disciplined, suspended, and eventually fired Ms. Nur for failure to remove her scarf. Several cases like Ms. Nur's have been brought to the courts to adjudicate claims of anti-Muslim discrimination in the context of the workplace and beyond. Women and girls who wear the headscarf or more concealing *niqab* (full covering, including face veil) for religious reasons have long been the subject of discrimination lawsuits; such suits have multiplied since 9/11.

A highly publicized post-9/11 bench trial in Florida, *Sultaana Lakiana Myke Freeman v. State of Florida*, involved a Muslim woman who wished to have her driver's license issued either without her photo on it or with a photo of her wearing dress that covered her entire body except for her eyes. Citing post-9/11 security concerns, the state of Florida insisted that the woman's driver's license is her primary form of identification and that law enforcement personnel ought to be able to determine the woman's identity efficiently with the aid of her license. A photoless license would not be very helpful in this endeavor, the state argued. The judge in this case agreed with the state, writing in her ruling that while the woman "most likely poses no threat to national security, there likely are people who would be willing to use a ruling permitting the wearing of full-face cloaks in driver's license photos by pretending to ascribe to religious beliefs in order to carry out activities that would threaten lives." The upshot of the court's ruling was that a Muslim woman was associated with the threat of terrorism simply on the basis of her appearance. While *she* is not a terrorist, the court said, others who intend to plot terrorist attacks might take advantage of the liberties protected by the Constitution to dress like this woman in order to disguise their identities. The reasoning on which this decision is based justifies state infringement of a fundamental liberty as a means to prevent a hypothetical crime in the future.

The ACLU has taken up the cause to fight against anti-Muslim "backlash" discrimination since September 11. The civil liberties organization is defending persons charged under the Patriot Act and other federal intelligence gathering laws with crimes related to espionage and terrorism. It has also defended Muslim women who have been discriminated against. For instance, in June 2004, the Nebraska chapter of the ACLU filed a civil rights lawsuit against the city of Omaha on behalf of Mrs. Lubna Hussein, a Muslim woman who was told she would have to take her headscarf and cloak off if she wanted to accompany her children at the municipal swimming pool. Pool employees told Mrs. Hussein that she could not be in the pool area with her "street clothes" on, even though she was not planning on swimming; Hussein observed that there were others in the pool area in street dress.

Hurtful Words to Physical Violence

Some incidents of anti-Muslim behavior actually involve violence or intrusive behavior on the part of the perpetrators. Amani al-Diffrawi, originally from Egypt, lived with her husband and four children in Torrance, California. She and her two daughters wore long dresses and headscarves when outside of their house. On September 27, 2000, al-Diffrawi's husband was out of town, and she and her children went to bed at 9:30 p.m. Soon thereafter she was awakened by loud pounding on her front door. Neighbors roused her to alert her that her house was on fire. Amani ran outside to discover a fire under the kitchen window of her house. Her neighbors helped her to douse the fire with a garden hose. Neighbors reported seeing a white male run up the driveway of al-Diffrawi's home to throw a Molotov cocktail, or incendiary device, against the house. The perpetrator, a Mr. Barrett, quickly escaped the scene in a white Ford pickup truck and was apprehended soon after by police. When they arrested him the perpetrator called the police officer a "nigger" and, when in the patrol car, made more racist remarks that were recorded on tape. He said, "I don't like other than whites and I will never change. . . ." When brought to trial the perpetrator testified that he disliked minorities. Asked how he felt about people from the Middle East, he said, "I wish they'd go home. I don't know any." He denied being the person who firebombed al-Diffrawi's house. Barrett was convicted of a hate crime by a jury.

The case of Samar Kaukab, a twenty-three-year-old U.S. citizen of Pakistani ancestry, born and raised in the United States, is worth examining in detail. Kaukab, who lives in Columbus, Ohio, and works for the national service program Volunteers in Service to America (VISTA), was detained at O'Hare Airport in Chicago on November 7, 2001, while passing through airport security. In accordance with her religious beliefs, she covers her hair and neck with a scarf at all times in public. At the airport she was wearing pants, a long sweater, and ankle-length boots as well as her *hijab* and carried a purse and a small bag.

While she was waiting in the security line, Kaukab noticed that occasionally someone would set off the metal detector. When this happened, the security staff did a quick, relatively nonintrusive additional search with a hand-held metal detector and then the person was allowed to go on his or her way. Kaukab saw a woman wearing a scarf on her head, and some people with baseball caps, walking through the checkpoint without being stopped or asked to remove their headgear. But none of these people, according to Kaukab, appeared to be of South Asian or Pakistani descent or wore clothing that would identify them as Muslim. Eventually, Kaukab sent her bags through the x-ray machine and walked through the metal detector without setting it off. When she went to retrieve her bags, however, a National Guardsman working for airport security instructed the security staff to stop and search her.

The security staff surrounded Kaukab as if to prevent her from leaving the checkpoint, and at the direction of Mr. Vargas, the National Guardsman, they searched her multiple times with a hand-held metal detector. A female security staff person passed the wand of the detector over Kaukab's head and upper body, down her legs and her crotch, and stuck the detector into her boots (while she was wearing them). She then conducted a pat-down, pulled the hooks and straps of Kaukab's bra, and asked Kaukab to lift her sweater. Despite numerous and extensive passes over Kaukab's head and body, the detector produced no audible signal. With a crowd beginning to gather, Kaukab felt embarrassed and humiliated.

After the female security staff completed the pat-down, the three staff members, after conferring with Vargas, ordered Kaukab to take off her headscarf. Kaukab explained she could not remove it in public for religious reasons. The staff insisted, and Kaukab stated that she would remove her headscarf in a private room or behind a screen and only in front of a woman. Her request was not honored. Feeling upset and violated, Kaukab repeatedly stated that for religious reasons she would not take off her *hijab* in public or in front of a man. After a lengthy discussion among the staff with Vargas, a male security guard ordered Kaukab to follow him to a room where he insisted that he search Kaukab while his female colleagues stood outside to guard the door. Kaukab, feeling harassed and frightened, repeated her objections. Finally the security staff agreed that Kaukab would go into the room with the two female security guards. . . .

Kaukab sued the commander of the Illinois National Guard and the airport security service provider contracted with United Airlines. She alleged that defendants violated her First Amendment rights to practice her religion, her Fourth Amendment right to be free from unreasonable searches, and her Fourteenth Amendment right to equal protection under the law. She also claimed that, because of her race, ancestry, color and/or ethnicity, the defendants deprived her of the full enjoyment of all the privileges, benefits, terms, and conditions of her passenger contract with United Airlines. Finally, she complained that the defendants falsely imprisoned her and committed battery against her....

As more Muslims immigrate to the United States, and more Muslim Americans take seriously the role that their religion might play in shaping their marriages and family life, American courts will be faced increasingly with instances of people blending or traversing between Islamic and domestic/civil sources of law.

Drawing New Lines

Western distortions and unfavorable portrayals of Islam and Muslims have been replete in popular culture and officialdom in the United States for many decades. Is a less-than-hospitable reception of Islamic legal norms in the courtrooms and law offices of the United States yet another example of this? Any Western discussion of Islamic family law necessarily begs the question of whether it condemns or misapprehends Islam as a religion and *shari'ah* as a body of law. As more Muslims immigrate to the United States, and more Muslim Americans take seriously the role that their religion might play in shaping their marriages and family life, American courts will be faced increasingly with instances of people blending or traversing between Islamic and domestic/civil sources of law. A desire by the courts to give Islamic law due respect draws the courts along the inevitable path of deciding what constitutes the appropriate interpretation of Islamic law to fit the particular circumstances before the courts, on a case-by-case basis. This may force courts into the impermissible terrain of violating the establishment clause, asking government officials to determine the content of religion.

Cases of divorce, discrimination in the workplace and schools, hate crimes, and passenger profiling in the aftermath of September 11, are all instances that display tensions between individual freedom and the authority of the state. The law is central in determining the relationship between the individual's right to religious liberty and the state's power to protect and promote such general interests as national security and gender equality. In some instances, we can see the state occasionally protecting a woman's right to wear a particular mode of dress despite resistance on the part of employers or schools who seek to promote other objectives. In other cases the state has acted in a manner that jeopardizes a woman's right to self-expression, by singling her out for extraordinary scrutiny and by making religious freedom secondary to competing interests. . . . For now, the *hijab* has made an easy symbol, both for the growing presence of Muslims and the increasing pluralism of public life in the United States. It may yet prove to be a harbinger of increasing toleration in the halls of justice.

9

Muslims Have a Right to Be Offended by Discrimination

Gary Younge

Gary Younge is the New York correspondent for the Guardian *(Manchester, U.K.) and the Alfred Knobler Journalism Fellow at the Nation Institute.*

The controversy over the cartoons published in 2005 in a Danish newspaper depicting the prophet Muhammad as a terrorist should serve as a warning to Americans. Discrimination against Muslims has risen dramatically since the terrorist attacks on September 11, 2001, and the First Amendment right of free speech does not give Americans the right to be offensive to others or to mock their beliefs.

In April 2003 Danish illustrator Christoffer Zieler submitted a series of unsolicited cartoons offering a lighthearted take on the resurrection of Christ to the Danish newspaper *Jyllands-Posten*. Zieler received an e-mail from the paper's Sunday editor, Jens Kaiser, saying: "I don't think *Jyllands-Posten*'s readers will enjoy the drawings. As a matter of fact, I think they will provoke an outcry. Therefore I will not use them." Two years later the same paper published twelve cartoons of Muhammad, including one with him wearing a turban shaped like a bomb with a burning fuse. Predictably enough, it created an outcry. How we got from there to talk of "the Muslim threat" to the immutable European traditions of secularism and freedom of speech, while Scandinavian embassies burn in the Arab world, is illuminating.

Four months after the cartoons were published, *Jyllands-Posten*'s editor apologized. In the intervening time Muslims engaged in mostly peaceful protests. Several Arab and Muslim nations withdrew their ambassadors from Denmark while demonstrators picketed embassies. According to Denmark's consul in Dubai, a boycott of Danish products in the Gulf would cost the country $27 million in sales.

All of this went largely unnoticed in the West, apart from critics who characterized the protests as evidence of a "clash of civilizations." In their attempt to limit free speech, went the argument, the demonstrators proved that Islam and Western democracy were incompatible.

Even on its own terms this logic is disingenuous. The right to offend must come with at least one consequent right and one subsequent responsibility. People must have the right to be offended, and those bold enough to knowingly cause offense should be bold enough to weather the consequences, so long as the aggrieved respond within the law. Muslims were in effect being vilified twice—once through the original cartoons and then again for having the gall to protest them. Such logic recalls the words of the late South African black nationalist Steve Biko: "Not only are whites kicking us; they are telling us how to react to being kicked."

Nonetheless, the "clash of civilizations" rhetoric framed the discussion for the almost inevitable violence to come. For as criticism mounted, other European newspapers decided to reprint the cartoons in solidarity with *Jyllands-Posten*. This was clearly inflammatory. Now the flames have reached all the way to the Middle East, where Danish and Norwegian embassies have been burned down. And the violence has been characterized as evidence that Muslims are plain uncivilized.

Freedom Does Not Justify Insensitivity

There seems to be almost universal agreement that these cartoons are offensive. There should also be universal agreement that the paper has a right to publish them without fear of violent reprisal. When it comes to freedom of speech, the liberal/left should not sacrifice its values one inch to those who seek censorship on religious grounds. But the right to freedom of speech equates to neither an obligation to offend nor a duty to be insensitive. If our commitment to free speech is important, our belief in antiracism should be no less so. Neither the cartoons nor the violence has emerged from a vacuum. They are steeped in and have contributed to an increasingly recriminatory atmosphere shaped by, among other things, war, intolerance and historic injustices. According to the Danish Institute for Human Rights, racially motivated crimes doubled in Denmark between 2004 and '05. These cartoons only served to compound Muslims' sense of alienation and vulnerability. The *Jerusalem Post* has now published the cartoons. Iranian newspaper *Hamshari* is calling for illustrators to ridicule the Holocaust. The race to the gutter is on.

There is nothing courageous about using your freedom of speech to ridicule the beliefs of one of the weakest sections of your society.

The acts of violence, including death threats to *Jyllands-Posten*'s editor, should be condemned. The fact remains, however, that the overwhelming swath of protests, particularly in Europe, where crass banners and suicide-bomber attire were the worst offenses, have so far been peaceful. But those who see this episode as freighted with weightier cultural meanings have another agenda. "This is a far bigger story than just the question of twelve cartoons in a small Danish newspaper," Flemming Rose, *Jyllands-Posten*'s culture editor, told the *New York Times*. Too right, but it is not the story Rose thinks it is. Rose claims that "this is about the question of integration and how compatible is the religion of Islam with a modern secular society." In the mistaken belief that Europe is a monoethnic continent to which nonwhite people have just arrived, Rose is not alone in refracting every protest by a minority through a racial, ethnic or religious lens.

In so doing he displays his ignorance of both modern secular society and the role of all religions within it. Without anything as explicit as a First Amendment, Europe's freedom of speech laws are far more piecemeal than those of the United States. Many were adopted as a result of the Holocaust—the most potent reminder of just how fragile and recent this liberal secular tradition truly is in Europe. Last year the French daily *Le Monde* was found guilty of "racist defamation" against Israel and the Jewish people. Madonna's book *Sex* was only unbanned in Ireland in 2004. Even as this debate rages, David Irving sits in jail in Austria charged with Holocaust denial over a speech he made seventeen years ago, Islamist cleric Abu Hamza has been convicted in London for incitement to murder and racial hatred and Louis Farrakhan remains banned from Britain because his arrival "would not be conducive to the public good." Even here in America school boards routinely ban the works of authors like Alice Walker and J.K. Rowling. Such actions should be opposed; but no one claims Protestant, Catholic or Jewish values are incompatible with democracy.

Which brings us back to Zieler. We will never know what the response to his Christ cartoons would have been because they were never published. (The paper's announced plan to reprint some cartoons about Christ fails to mitigate its double standard.) That fact alone shows that the question has never been whether you draw a line under what is or isn't acceptable to publish, but where you draw it. There is nothing courageous about using your freedom of speech to ridicule the beliefs of one of the weakest sections of your society. But Rose and others like him clearly believe Muslims, by virtue of their religion, exist on the wrong side of the line. That exclusion finds its reflection in the Islamist rejection of all things Western. And so the secularists and antiracists in both the West and the Middle East find their space for maneuver limited, while dogma masquerades as principle, and Islamists and Islamophobes are confirmed in their own vile prejudices.

10

Discrimination Against Muslims Is Highly Exaggerated

Daniel Mandel

Daniel Mandel is a fellow in history at Melbourne University, an author, and the director of the Zionist Organization of America's Center for Middle East Policy.

The claims that discrimination against Muslims has increased dramatically since the terrorist acts on September 11, 2001, are, at best, exaggerations and at worst, blatant lies. The majority of hate-crime complaints and lawsuits were dismissed because there was no evidence on which to base the accusations. The media have become overly cautious in their attempt to avoid discriminating against Muslims in the United States and are even distorting facts to cater to a minority of the American population.

Spokesmen for Muslim groups in the West have made a large number and wide variety of claims against the societies in which they live. They speak of racism and discrimination, with the alleged misdeeds they cite ranging from defamation in the media and in Hollywood to physical attacks.

Capitol Hill and the White House seem to think these claims have a basis in fact. After the terrorist attacks of September 11, 2001, the Senate passed a resolution condemning "any acts of violence or discrimination against any Americans, including Arab Americans and American Muslims"; shortly thereafter, George W. Bush warned that intimidation of Muslims "should not and . . . will not stand in America." Presidents and Senates don't make statements of that type without believing that the situation calls for them. But does it?

If America were in the grip of anti-Muslim ferment, we could expect to see a major increase in hate crimes against Muslims and a corresponding lack of receptiveness to Muslim entreaties in the government, the media, and the public. According to a number of Muslim and Arab advocacy organizations, this is precisely what is happening.

The Council on American-Islamic Relations (CAIR), in "Unequal Protection," its civil-rights report for 2005, provides several graphs registering dramatic increases in reported civil-rights and hate-crimes cases: 1,522 civil-rights cases in 2004, up from 1,019 in 2003 and 602 in 2002; and 141 "actual and potential" hate crimes in 2004, as against 93 in 2003 and 42 in 2002. The Arab-American Anti-Discrimination Committee (ADC) too, in its 2001–2002 report on hate crimes, alleged 165 violent incidents from January to October of 2002, amounting to a "significant increase over most years in the past decade."

Fact Versus Fiction

The reality is rather different. Fabricated incidents and frivolous complaints have abounded in these reports and others like them. For example, no fewer than five cases of arson or vandalism of Muslim businesses appear to have been the result of attempted insurance fraud on the part of the businesses' owners. In two cases, CAIR protested on behalf of those alleging hate crimes, Mirza Akram and Amjad Abunar, demanding investigations—and then was struck dumb when each man was charged with arson. Other incidents reported by CAIR cannot be substantiated. There are no police records to back up the alleged explosion of a bomb outside a Houston mosque in July 2004. Another case CAIR cites—a mosque fire in Springfield, Mass.—was eventually ruled to be a juvenile robbery in which the fire was lit to obliterate evidence of a break-in, and was not motivated by anti-Muslim bias. Past ADC reports have referred to egg-pelting incidents against Muslims on a university campus that, on inspection, proved in one case not to have had an obvious hateful motive, and in the other to have been a fabrication by the supposed victim.

Turning to the most serious crime—murder—of eight reported by CAIR in the year following September 11, 2001, all but one had ambiguous motives and on investigation could not be attributed to anti-Muslim motivation. More recently, Daniel Pipes and Sharon Chadha took a microscope to some incidents in CAIR's latest report and concluded that, of "twenty 'anti-Muslim hate crimes' in 2004 that CAIR describes, at least six are invalid." Findings like these fatally compromise the credence that can be paid to CAIR's reports.

Corporations too have been obsequious, perhaps because commerce is highly sensitive to organizations willing and able to trumpet claims of discrimination and insensitivity.

Beyond citing examples that appear to be outright fabrications, the authors of CAIR's reports show a remarkable ingenuity in defining what constitutes an expression of anti-Muslim bias. Hollywood has been a particular target of Muslim groups for its supposed insensitivity. The ADC decries "the extremely serious problem of negative stereotyping of Arabs and Arab Americans in the entertainment industry." With metronomic regularity, Muslim groups protest action films dealing with Middle Eastern terrorists for reinforcing a supposed culture of intolerance and racism. To Westerners, they present their argument as an appeal for fair play. Elsewhere—particularly in the Middle East—their complaint takes on an anti-Semitic complexion—the culprit now being conscienceless Jewish domination of a Hollywood that slavishly serves the interests of Israel, or of the U.S. military-industrial complex, or whatever variant thereof the subject and occasion demand.

Walking on Eggshells

In fact, nothing very sinister is afoot. Hollywood has always dealt in a range of stock characters and situations, and this is not reprehensible when it has a basis in fact. It is not malignity, but reality, that leads filmmakers to depict Nazis as Germans or World War II Japanese generals as imperialists. Likewise, documentaries and films on terrorism that are inspired by actual events tend to tell Middle Eastern, not Scandinavian, stories. If anything, Hollywood has latterly gone to extraordinary lengths to avoid offending Muslims, dragging other groups into service as terrorist villains. In *The Sum of All Fears*, the Middle Eastern terrorists of Tom Clancy's novel were transformed, following CAIR's intercession with the director, into European neo-Nazis. In *The Interpreter*, sub-Saharan Africans replaced the Muslims originally intended as terrorist villains. Recently, Fox acceded to CAIR's concerns over an episode of its [television] series *24* that depicted Muslim terrorists by announcing it would give airtime to CAIR for public-service messages.

> *On any serious index of hate crimes and discrimination against Muslims, Americans are not significantly represented.*

Hollywood's pusillanimity in the face of criticism from Muslim groups mirrors a sometimes misplaced sensitivity and presumption of guilt displayed by other institutions. CAIR is a Saudi-funded organization whose founder is on record praising suicide bombers and saying he would like the Koran to be the highest authority in America, and whose personnel have been implicated in crimes consistent with these positions. One would expect that, with such a record, CAIR would be shunned. To the contrary, it is courted by government, law-enforcement agencies, civil-liberties groups, and religious bodies. Corporations too have been obsequious, perhaps because commerce is highly sensitive to organizations willing and able to trumpet claims of discrimination and insensitivity. As a result, Arabic-script logos deemed offensive to Muslims have been removed by advertisers; a broadcaster who offended CAIR has been fired; and Internet providers have taken down websites filled with content hostile to Islam—something unlikely to occur in respect of anti-Jewish hate sites.

It is something of an Islamist triumph that such a weak case for corrective action has drawn such wide support in a country where Muslims have done exceedingly well. For the truth is that American society is generally respectful of Muslim needs and concerns. Muslim men and women who have lost their jobs for violating employer dress codes (by insisting on beards or traditional garb), or who have suffered even inadvertent discrimination in the workplace, have been either generously compensated or reinstated. Conversely, other groups suffering more from hate crimes tend to get ignored. In 2004, the FBI reported 1,374 crimes motivated by religious bias, of which 954 (67.8 percent) were committed against Jews, but only 156 (12.7 percent) against Muslims. This has not resulted in allegations of an anti-Jewish crime wave in the United States, much less in concerted action to address pervasive racism against Jews.

On any serious index of hate crimes and discrimination against Muslims, Americans are not significantly represented. We should remember this truth next time complaints emerge from CAIR and likeminded groups. In particular, the mainstream media should treat these claims without credulity and independently verify allegations; government and institutions should shun radical pressure groups; and corporations, perhaps the most vulnerable target of campaigns alleging racism and insensitivity, should deploy strategies other than caving in.

11

Discrimination Against Muslims in America Must Stop

Rajmohan Gandhi

Rajmohan Gandhi is the grandson of Mohandas Gandhi and delivered this speech at the tenth anniversary celebration of Richmond, Virginia's, Unity Walk of 1993.

America has always been a changing nation, willing to admit to its mistakes and make atonement for injustices. Just as the segregation between blacks and whites was wrong and has been outlawed, so now the segregation between Muslims and non-Muslims must end. Reconciliation is the key to making progress and eliminating discrimination in America.

Let me start by reading a quote from Thomas Jefferson that I am sure many here can recite from memory. Though the quote is not directly related to our purpose this evening, it has some relevance. Said Jefferson:

> Believing that religion is a matter which lies solely between man and his God, ... I contemplate with sovereign reverence that act of the whole American people which declared that their Legislature should "make no law respecting an establishment of religion, or prohibiting the free exercise thereof," thus building a wall of separation between Church and State.

Thomas Jefferson of Virginia is known throughout the world as the architect of this wall of separation between

Rajmohan Gandhi, "A Pact Between Man and His God," *Vital Speeches of the Day*, vol. 70, February 1, 2004. Reproduced by permission of the author.

church and state, a wall that has protected stability and democracy in several nations. I cannot help feeling that thanks to the decade-long commitment of the kind of people gathered this evening, Richmond and Virginia will also become known for breaking down the wall of separation between communities; and that this demonstration too will help stability and democracy in places far from here.

Making History

When, ten years ago, I had the privilege, along with a great many others, to walk for unity through Richmond's acknowledged and often-painful past, and when, like the others, I felt greatly moved, I also sensed that history was not only being experienced in a fresh way—history was being made. This evening's gathering, setting, and spirit suggest to me that that sense of the starting of a new history was not false—that the people of Richmond have embraced the processes of honest conversation and healing the past, with the involvement, if possible, of every sector and every individual.

As a citizen of the world I therefore salute and thank the people and leaders of Richmond. While doing so, I also offer my respect to America as a whole, for Richmond's initiatives are characteristic of America as a whole.

To me America encourages the death of hierarchy, and the breath of equal opportunity.

No country is perfect, yet I am struck by America's ability to keep changing. When I first visited America in 1957, it was a white country, with Blacks living silently, anonymously, invisibly. They were in the wings, while white America was on the stage. Billboards, TV commercials, and newspaper ads showed only white faces.

A tiny hint of color-based discrimination reached me when in 1957 I walked across a Detroit suburb for a haircut. Entering, one after the other, three barber shops, I was told in each of them that they did not have cutters for my thick hair; I believed them until I heard that excuse for the third time.

Understanding the Need for Change

I visited the USA after a fourteen-year gap, and met a different country and saw a different landscape. A white country had become a white-and-black country. Now, in 2003, almost every representation of America, on billboards, TV ads, or anywhere, lets you know that this is a white-black-Hispanic-Asian-and-more country. You do not now see a single-color or even a two-color image of America.

In August this year, on [nonprofit political TV network] C-SPAN, I heard Beppe Severgnini, the Italian author of *Ciao, America* name a few positive American traits: optimism, a sense of responsibility, direct answers, and a sense that rules are meant to be obeyed. On optimism, he said that Americans work to win but are ready to lose; if they lose they try again or try another thing.

My own reactions to America are similar. On responsibility, I find here that the level of responsibility seems to go up as you go down the hierarchy. It seems to me that the American at the base, the bus driver, the post office worker, the firefighters accepts and practices almost complete responsibility. To me America encourages the death of hierarchy, and the breath of equal opportunity.

A person of insight, or a person with a large heart, finds equals everywhere. As [American poet] Walt Whitman wrote: "I have looked for equals and lovers and found them ready for me in all lands; I think some divine rapport has equalized me with them." But even ordinary mortals, with limited hearts, encounter the attitude of equality when they land in the USA.

America Is Everyone's Country

I have found that America is everyone's country. You are an American not because you have the right bloodline, the same ancestor as others, but very often simply by being in America. I am from India, I hold an Indian passport, sometimes I criticize U.S. policies, but colleagues, students, and staff at the University of Illinois, and others I run into in the twin cities of Urbana and Champaign, treat me as one of them. As far as they are concerned, I am an American because I am here. I doubt that there is any other country like this.

Yes, if you are a visitor you Americanize in some ways, your pronunciation and accent change, even if you are all of 68 years; your language changes; maybe your appearance also changes. As [Italian journalist Beppe] Severgnini said, you begin to wear a baseball cap; then, after six months, you turn it 180 degrees on your head. Your American-ness is a matter of residence, and your nationality, if you become an American, is a matter of laws not of genes. At least it is a matter not of genes with a G, only of jeans with a J.

This quickly-offered American-ness is something new and rare and precious in the world. It has to be protected jealously.

The Great Divide

When 9/11 occurred, I was in my home just south of New Delhi, in India. My sister phoned asking me to turn the TV on, as buildings in New York, she said, had been attacked. Like the rest of the world, I spent most of the hours that followed, horrified and shocked, in front of a TV set, and my heart flew to America. As a British writer has recently put it, that day love flew to America from all over the world.

9/11 dried up the oceans and joined the U.S. to the soil of the earth as a whole; America lost its safety, its separateness, its sense of being specially protected; it became one with all of vulnerable humanity. On the other hand, 9/11 also made America more fearful of the world, or at least of large sections of the world.

Neither the West nor the Muslim world is by any means a homogeneous entity. Yet the division between what is seen as the West and what is seen as the Muslim world is perhaps the most critical divide the modern world has faced.

Both sides in this divide claim to worship God and to honor the value of equality. The world's Muslims insist that Islam is almost above all the religion of equality. There is God at one level, merciful and compassionate and almighty, and there is, at a lower level, humanity, where, Muslims say, all humans are equal, irrespective of race, or class, or gender, or nationality.

The West says the same; America says the same. All are created equal, that is America's solemn oath. It is a belief expressed at every level. President [George W.] Bush has said again and again that in his belief all are equal in the eyes of God, and that all human lives have equal value.

Grave Misunderstandings

And yet, voices in the Islamic world portray America as a Satan or a devil; and some voices in the West, including America, present Islam as a uniquely flawed religion and Muslims as a flawed people.

For any Christians or Jews to defame Islam is therefore to defame siblings—some extremely cultivated and fine siblings at that.

If I were a Muslim, or living in a Muslim land, I would wonder at the sanity of anyone calling America satanic. This America that has offered space, opportunity and freedom of worship to millions of Muslims from other lands, where Muslims can practice their faith and claim a share in the running of America, an America that defended the rights of the Muslims of Bosnia and Kosovo, and supported the Mujahideen of Afghanistan in their courageous struggle against Soviet rule in the 1980s, this America may make mistakes, and may at times hurt the feelings of many people, but to call this America satanic is not only to utter a terrible untruth, it is also the surest way of keeping the Muslim world insulated from the progress of humankind.

And what about those who would tell America that Islam is evil? Fortunately, they are in a minority. Some days ago I heard a talk at the University of Illinois by a distinguished scholar from Emory University, Atlanta, Professor Vernon Robbins. Comparing Al Fateha, the opening chapter of the Qur'an, to the Lord's Prayer, Professor Robbins showed that the two short texts had similar sentiments and a similar structure, and he described some of the continuities of the Abrahamic tradition, common to Christianity and Islam, that may account for the remarkable similarities in the two remarkable texts.

Rejecting Family

For any Christians or Jews to defame Islam is therefore to defame siblings—some extremely cultivated and fine siblings at that. It is also, of course, hazardous in a very practical sense. Muslims and non-Muslims live next to one another or among one another in scores of countries in varying degrees of trust and tension—in India, in Indonesia, in Bangladesh, in the Philippines, in Nigeria, in South Africa, in Egypt, in Lebanon, in Cyprus, in many countries of Europe, in Russia, China, and in the USA, and right here in Richmond. To spread the notion that Muslims are especially dangerous is to risk tension, division and violence in a number of places.

But there is a deeper question here. Most Muslims are Muslims because they were born into Muslim families; most Americans are Americans because they were born so. Blaming Muslims because they are Muslim, or Americans because they are American, means that people are being condemned, for their birth, for their blood, for their DNA.

Despite all that the world has learned of the horror of condemning people for their birth, for being born to their parents, despite the horrors of the Holocaust, of slavery, of untouchability in India, we seem willing yet again to target a section of human beings for being who they are, for being Muslims or Americans.

It seems that the world needs again a Martin Luther King, Jr., or a Gandhi, or a Lincoln. America can do with men and women of that sort, and the Islamic world can do with them.

It is true that the 9/11 attackers called themselves Muslims, and some of them may have conducted their attack in the name of Islam. Some of the killings in Rwanda in 1994 were conducted inside churches. All the killers (and the victims too) were Christians. Did that make the Rwandan killings a Christian crime? When Hindus and Buddhists are involved in terrible deeds in Sri Lanka, are we to blame Hinduism and Buddhism? Nazism and Communism were enthroned, and the Holocaust carried out, in supposedly Christian lands. Are we therefore to impute a great flaw to Christianity?

The Need for Unity

Slavery was practiced, and also apartheid, in Christian societies and often in the name of Christianity. Did the slaves blame Christianity? Were the spirituals anti-Christian? Did Nelson Mandela strive to alert his people in South Africa to an evil inherent in Christianity?

It seems that the world needs again a Martin Luther King, Jr., or a Gandhi, or a Lincoln. America can do with men and women of that sort, and the Islamic world can do with them. If King were around today, and living by chance as a citizen of a Muslim country, he would ask his people to oppose American policies that they thought were wrong, but he would warn his people against the folly of hating America or Americans. He would speak truth to power and also to the street. He would tell the Arab street, and the youth, and the religious teachers, that while violence would invite harsh reprisals on the weakest among them, nonviolent initiatives would surprise the opponent and could defeat him.

May King find spiritual descendants in the Muslim world, and in the USA. I will speak about Gandhi, too, but let me first offer a thought or two about [Abraham] Lincoln. Here I must say that it is a little miracle that in the Tredegar Gun Foundry we can now comfortably speak of Lincoln. In September, I saw on TV the conversation that Brit Hume of Fox News had with President Bush in the White House. In the Oval Office, Hume asked the President about the sources of his inspiration. President Bush named Lincoln, and pointed to the Lincoln portrait in the room. When Hume asked how Lincoln inspired him, the President said that in a time of civil war Lincoln fought for American unity. After 9/11, the President continued, he too felt called, in the spirit of Lincoln, to invoke unity in the United States.

Avoid Judging Others

I think it is good to ask what Lincoln, if he were alive today, would have said. We can never know for certain, of course, yet it is perhaps useful to try. All here know the timeless lines from the Second Inaugural. Referring to the two sides in the war that saw ceaseless activity in this space, Lincoln said:

> Both read the same Bible, and pray to the same God; and each invokes his aid against the other. It may seem strange that any men should dare to ask a just God's assistance in wringing their bread from the sweat of other men's faces, but let us judge not, that we be not judged.

As I look at these lines, I feel that today they speak not to two sides inside America, but to two forces appearing to clash in the world, the West led by the USA, and the Muslim world; and the challenge that Lincoln today might pose, a challenge that King, Jefferson, and Gandhi too might today pose, is not merely the attainment of American unity, but the healing of the larger global divide I have referred to.

I leave it to the audience to decide whether "making God an accomplice in a wicked deed," focusing on the religion of the attackers and claiming divine injunctions to destroy the wicked are relevant questions.

After 9/11, which joined America to the suffering soil of the rest of our earth, Americans cannot afford to think only of uniting America—though, given today's sharp divisions in the USA, that too is a vital goal. Americans certainly can do with honest and respectful conversations with one another. Yet after 9/11, America, and all of us, have to strive to heal and unite the world, and for a just and lasting peace everywhere, including in the Middle East. . . .

A Longing for Reconciliation

I leave it to the audience to decide whether "making God an accomplice in a wicked deed," focusing on the religion of the attackers, and claiming divine injunctions to destroy the wicked are relevant questions in November 2003.

I know that I am preaching to the choir. Those assembled here are practitioners of reconciliation, men and women who have had a part in connecting communities; men and women who know that while the examples of persons like King, Lincoln and Gandhi can on occasion restore our spirits, what matters in the end is the part that each of us is willing to play.

Finally, let me share a small story. It is about a long time ago—1956. But if you invite a man my age you risk hearing of a long time ago.

1956 was the year in which I made my first trip ever to the Western world. I traveled from India to Europe and Britain. That year Britain, France, and Israel attacked Egypt. (The USA, I should point out, had opposed the attack.) I was 21, and independent India was but nine years old. I felt that the attack on Egypt was a revival of imperialism.

I became bitter. I was conscious of my feelings as I saw the great castles, palaces, and museums of Europe, admired what I saw, and yet resented what I saw. I would have been glad to see some damage done to what I was looking at.

Mercifully, the ill-will left me after some months. I think it left me because of the kind of people I met in Europe and Britain. They were ordinary people yet wonderful people, decent, interested in me as a person, honest about their humanity and their human failures, involved in assisting other people. I could not continue to dislike people like that! I would have lost any respect for myself if I had continued to nurse my ill-will. Before long I also realized that I too, was capable of wanting to force my will on others, even as I felt Egypt had been pressurized. You might say that I saw the European in me, and myself in the European.

I am sure we have all had similar experiences, and we have known of similar experiences in the world around us. A longing for reconciliation is perhaps programmed into our minds. Reconciliation is part of the great American story; it is the story we celebrate this evening; it is our vision for the world.

12

Homosexuality Causes Religious Discrimination Within the Episcopal Church

S.C. Gwynne

S.C. Gwynne is a writer for Texas Monthly.

The vote at the General Convention of the Episcopal Church in August 2003, which approved the ordination of a homosexual bishop, has led to a division between liberal and conservative Episcopalians so deep that both sides fear the entire denomination could split. There is discrimination against homosexuals and those who support their choice, and a debate over what Scripture has to say about the issue.

In the priesthood of the Episcopal Church, the Reverend Canon David H. Roseberry has long been considered something of a prodigy. In 1985 he founded Christ Church in a Plano [Texas] home with a mere 13 people and quickly built it into a powerhouse with 4,400 members and a 500-student Sunday school. It has the largest average Episcopal church attendance in America and is the most successful start-up in the denomination's history. It is also deeply conservative, heavily tilted toward Scripture, and determinedly evangelical. In its striking growth, its many successful outreach programs, and its broad community involvement, Christ Church is precisely what the national church, whose membership has been steadily declining for the past forty years, aspires to be.

S.C. Gwynne, "Peace Be with You," *Texas Monthly*, vol. 32, July 2004. Reproduced by permission.

But on Sunday, August 10, 2003, Roseberry stood in the pulpit of his vaulted limestone sanctuary and delivered a rhetorical cruise missile directed at the heart of his denomination. Five days earlier, bishops from 107 dioceses at the church's triennial General Convention, in Minneapolis, had voted to consecrate the ordination of a homosexual bishop named V. Gene Robinson in New Hampshire and to approve the blessing of same-sex unions. To Roseberry, this meant that the church had ignored the Bible and thus, on this issue, had abandoned the Christian faith. "In two days, in two votes by less than six hundred people, 4,500 years of Biblical teaching and tradition were overturned," he told the congregation. Then he explained why he had walked off the convention floor in protest. "I wanted to send the very clearest, least ambiguous signal to you that I will not be pushed or pulled into an apostate church. I can't do it. These things are too important to me, and it's too much of a violation of what I believe and hold sacred." He received a standing ovation that lasted almost a full minute.

In the weeks that followed, Roseberry became one of the main organizers of an unprecedented revolt against the national church. It began in conservative parishes like Christ Church and in dioceses like Dallas, Fort Worth, and Pittsburgh, Pennsylvania, and quickly spread through the global Anglican communion. (The Episcopal Church is the American name of the Anglican Church, which was created by Henry VIII after he split with the Roman Catholic Church, in 1534; Anglican churches now operate in 164 countries and have 73 million members.) Episcopalians suddenly found themselves in the middle of a bloody, media-fueled political fight. The church had long tolerated the presence of gay priests, and some bishops had been ordaining openly gay priests and deacons since the eighties. But to many members, a gay bishop was unthinkable. Conservative parishes announced that they were leaving the denomination and were promptly sued by their dioceses for their land and buildings. Some congregations just walked away, en masse, from their property. Whole dioceses and hundreds of parishes announced that they would no longer give money to the national church. In Texas, the home of some of the church's most conservative clergy, the backlash was especially severe. All of its five bishops had voted against Robinson; four of them publicly condemned the vote. "As faithful Episcopalians, we grieve with other Christians who are shocked and offended by these decisions," wrote Fort Worth bishop Jack Leo Iker in a furious pastoral letter that his 56 vicars and rectors were ordered to read aloud from the pulpit. At St. Michael's Church in Richland Hills, in Iker's diocese, the rector threw the flag of the national church on the ground and then walked on it in protest. In March six conservative retired bishops, led by former Diocese of Texas bishop Maurice Benitez, broke canon law by holding confirmations in Ohio without the permission of the bishop there: the confirmands had refused to be blessed by a bishop who voted for Robinson. (To a lesser extent, the same thing is happening in other Protestant denominations, including the Presbyterian and Methodist churches; but they have had nothing like an official endorsement of a gay bishop.)

The Conflict Heightens

The most telling event in the conflict was an October meeting of the Episcopal Church's leading dissidents, called by Roseberry and organized by Christ Church. Roseberry was in a unique position: He led a congregation that was more uniformly conservative than perhaps any other in the nation, and he was ensconced in what was certifiably one of the most conservative dioceses in the country—Dallas. He had initially expected to draw 200 to 300 people. To his amazement, he got 2,800, including, stunningly, 40 bishops among 900 clergymen. The meeting was so large that it had to be moved from Christ Church to the Wyndham Anatole Hotel, in Dallas, and it quickly showed the rest of the world the depth and strength of the conservative protest. "It was an exclamation point in the life of the Episcopal Church," says Roseberry. "We were saying, 'Wow, this is the defining moment for all of us.'"

That led to another meeting in January, again organized by Roseberry's church and this time held on its campus. There the simmering dissent of October turned to incipient schism. Thirteen bishops and representatives from twelve dioceses around the country (including Dallas and Fort Worth) and various conservative parishes formed an alliance representing some 10 percent of the church. They called it the Network of Anglican Communion Dioceses and Parishes (known as the Network). Their purpose was to form a sort of church within the church, with its own "moderator" and a missionary focus. The Network would resist the ordination of gays and minister to the conservative congregations who now refused to take communion with presiding bishop Frank Griswold, the head of the church—or to even have him visit their churches. Such a deliberate challenge to Episcopal leadership was without precedent, and it convinced many in the clergy and the laity that sooner or later the church would shatter on a scale unseen in its 215-year history.

> *What is inarguably true is that . . . the Episcopal Church in America is in serious decline. Some would say it is a fatal decline.*

The problem extends well beyond the borders of the United States. The larger, and starker, truth of the American rebellion is that while the bishops of Dallas and Fort Worth, whose dioceses have joined the Network, are in the minority of American Episcopal leaders opposed to having a gay bishop, they are in the overwhelming majority in the rest of the Anglican world. Of the Anglican Church's 38 provinces around the globe, 21 have already declared themselves in "impaired" or "broken" communion with the American church. Archbishop Peter Akinola, of Nigeria, whose 17.5 million members dwarf the 2.3 million members of the Episcopal Church in America, roundly condemned the General Convention's vote and called it "a Satanic attack." And even in the relatively more liberal United States, 42 percent of the bishops voted against Robinson. If joining the Network means a falling out of communion with the Episcopal Church, it means a strengthening of ties with the rest of the world.

It is difficult to see just where this revolt is headed or how far it will go. For conservatives, the vote means the end of what's left of the old, scripturally driven church as they have known it. For liberals, it marks a triumph in a 28-year religious battle and the beginning of a new world of social and divine justice. What is inarguably true is that while the Anglican Church is booming in Africa, Asia, and Latin America, the Episcopal Church in America is in serious decline. Some would say it is a fatal decline. It has lost nearly a third of its membership in the past 40 years, and as a percentage of the U.S. population, the number of Episcopal Church members has dropped from 1.8 percent, in 1960, to .75 percent today. The fight over how to address homosexuality in the church is also, rather obviously, a fight about how to save it.

Progressive Episcopalians Gain Ground

In the city of Dallas, fifteen miles south of David Roseberry's airy $8 million sanctuary, is a much older and smaller Episcopal church called St. Thomas the Apostle. St. Thomas is also well known inside the national church, but for different reasons. In the eighties it began ministering to people with HIV and soon became known as the "AIDS church." "We were serving the spiritual needs of sick people," says the church's rector, Father Stephen Waller. "A lot of people were dying. A lot of our members went to God. For fifteen years we were burying people hand over fist. Because of that, this once sleepy parish became a magnet for gay and lesbian people."

St. Thomas is by no means a typical Episcopal church. It is as liberal as Christ Church is conservative. But unlike Christ Church, St. Thomas is in the mainstream of the Episcopal Church in 2004. Gene Robinson's consecration, after all, signaled a victory for liberals in a long war. Waller, who is gay, is nonetheless in the difficult position of leading a majority gay and lesbian church in one of the most conservative dioceses in the country, presided over by one of the nation's most conservative bishops, the Right Reverend James M. Stanton. Waller's congregation—their sexual preferences aside—are like church members anywhere: They sit on the vestry (the church's governing board), sing in the choir, teach Sunday school, read the Bible, bring groceries to shut-ins, and perform as lay readers on Sunday. Because the liberal side of the Episcopal Church has long held that their sexual practices are not sinful, there is nothing, theologically speaking, special about them. Waller says that while most members of his parish were "delighted" by the vote of the General Convention, they were also horrified when their diocese joined the conservative Network five months later. The vestry of the church protested by writing a letter to Stanton saying that it "disassociates itself" from the decision to join the Network and that it would not give the Network money. In his church newsletter, Waller wrote, "I do not choose to be part of any group the purpose of which is to purify God's church or any group whose function is to claim to be some sort of faithful remnant of 'right' believers in America."

Homosexuality was just one area in which conservatives thought the church increasingly weak and more reflective of American pop culture than the Bible.

Waller's status as an outsider in his diocese is underscored by his willingness to bless same-sex unions, against both traditional church policy and the wishes of his bishop. "I have spoken to the bishop on several occasions about this issue," says Waller, "Last year, after our diocesan convention, it was decided officially that we would not bless same-sex relationships. I had done some. I drove to his office and told him that I do them but that I would not do it if he did not want it done. I told him he is still my bishop. We agreed to disagree. He was graceful enough. I said I was deeply saddened." (The General Convention last August gave local bishops the authority to approve same-sex unions for the first time; before that, it was against the rules of the church.)

Not a New Problem

Though Robinson's consecration brought such tensions into a new and sharper focus they have long existed inside the church. Starting in the early seventies, variations of this theological debate about homosexuality kept breaking out at Episcopal diocesan and national conventions. As always, the subtext was how the church interpreted Scripture. Homosexuality was just one area in which conservatives thought the church increasingly weak and more reflective of American pop culture than the Bible. There were also growing numbers of liberals who challenged the Resurrection, the Virgin Birth, and the Holy Trinity and who believed the Bible to be more of a loose metaphorical guideline than divinely inspired truth. Powerful conservative groups such as Episcopalians United and the American Anglican Communion sprang up to push back. The breaking point—and one of the most significant events in church history—came in the heresy trial of Bishop Walter Righter in 1996. At issue was the 1990 ordination of a gay deacon in the diocese of Newark, New Jersey, home of the articulate, iconoclastic leader of the church's liberal wing, the Right Reverend John S. Spong, who was then its bishop. Righter was Spong's assistant.

Spong had ordained a gay priest in late 1989 and had deliberately publicized it. The church's bishops voted to censure him—but by a tepid majority of 80–76. Attitudes in the church were changing; liberals were gaining ground. Gay ordinations continued in the diocese of Newark, and in 1996 conservatives in the church decided to take a stand by trying Righter on two charges stemming from his 1990 ordination of an avowedly gay deacon, both of which involved a violation of ordination laws. The result was a decision by the bishops in the trial court that sent shock waves through the Anglican world. They ruled that the church had no "core doctrine" on sexuality that prohibited the ordination of a gay priest. Just how far to the left of the rest of the Anglican world this put the American church became clear in 1998, at the Anglican Church's Lambeth Conference, a once-a-decade meeting of church leaders in England. Bishops voted 562–70 for a resolution declaring that while gays were "loved by God," homosexual activity was "incompatible with Scripture" and advising against the ordination of non-celibate gays. Most of the 70 dissenters, of course, came from the increasingly isolated American church.

It was one thing to have gay priests, whom conservatives do not approve of but consider to be aberrations . . . and quite another to have an avowedly gay bishop.

Still, until last summer's vote, the Episcopal Church had seemed to weather the controversy, just as it had previous disputes over the ordination of women (1976) and prayer book reform (1979)—both of which passed with relatively small net effect on church membership. Its factions were still deeply divided, but the church had not changed its official policy—disapproval—on homosexual clergy. The 2003 General Convention vote changed that irrevocably. In spite of his own ability to come to a somewhat wary accommodation with Bishop Stanton, Stephen Waller is among many priests who believe that the larger church is unlikely to remain whole. "For anyone in the Episcopal Church who has half a heart," he says, "it is very difficult to watch as we chew each other up. I think the church is headed for a split, and that causes me enormous sadness. The question is how we keep the others aboard the ship."

Common Misconceptions

Considering the fact that many Episcopal churches have long made gays feel welcome, just what is it that conservatives can't abide about homosexuals? And in a church that has knowingly ordained homosexual priests at least since the seventies, what was it about the consecration of a bishop in the tiny diocese of New Hampshire in 2003 that touched off such a global storm in the Anglican Church? The church's conservative wing says that the dispute is about two, and only two, issues: the church's adherence to Scripture and the church's adherence to its own historical teachings. They argue, with little credible opposition, that the Bible consistently condemns gay sex. It is, as they like to say, "univocal" on the subject, from Genesis to Leviticus to Paul's letters to the Corinthians. In all, the subject is mentioned only eight times and never by Jesus himself. "What we believe is based on Scripture and also on the unbroken practice of the Christian church and our Jewish forefathers for five millennia," says Fort Worth's Jack Iker, one of the most conservative bishops in the church and one of three who still refuse to ordain women to the priesthood. "The church has always been unanimous in its condemnation of the homosexual lifestyle. The cultures that the Christian church came into—Roman and Greek—were very firmly accepting of homosexuality, and men having sexual relationships with young boys was common and acceptable, especially for the upper classes. But the church, coming out of its Jewish heritage, was very much countercultural that way."

It is a common misconception that conservatives like Iker, Stanton, and Roseberry want to exclude gays from the church altogether. This is not what they say, and there is no evidence that it is true. (They are even agreeable to being part of a church that ordains homosexuals, as they have proven for more than two decades.) Their position is that Scripture holds homosexual acts to be unnatural, ungodly, and therefore sinful. The foundation of that belief—necessarily—is that homosexuality is a behavioral choice. Like any behavioral choice, it can be resisted. Like any temptation to sin, it needs to be resisted. And like other sinners, conservatives say, gays are welcomed into the church to worship and receive God's love and forgiveness. "As an individual, you should know that if you are an active member of a gay lifestyle, that is outside of God's will," says Roseberry. "It is an unnatural, broken love, and it is not God's best for you. It is God's call in your life to bring every aspect of your life under his lordship. And so if there is divorce, repentance; if there is homosexual attraction, celibacy; if there is homosexual sin, repentance; if there is heterosexual sin or attraction to someone outside of your marriage, repentance." Still, it was one thing to have gay priests, whom conservatives do not approve of but consider to be aberrations, products of ecclesiastical lawlessness, and quite another to have an avowedly gay bishop, which represented a doctrinal change. A gay bishop meant that the church no longer believed that homosexual behavior was sinful.

The Other Side of the Coin

Liberals make several basic counterarguments. The most basic is that the sexual preference of gays is not a "behavior" that they choose and therefore cannot be a sin like other chosen behaviors, such as adultery. (Both sides say that science upholds their claims.) Perhaps the most common argument is that committed, monogamous homosexual relationships did not exist in biblical times and therefore were never addressed. Most of the Bible's depictions of homosexuality are indeed either predatory or exploitative in some way. "If you take what Paul's letters and Leviticus and Genesis say about homosexuality, it is like comparing pornography or XXX video places to committed heterosexual relationships," says Barbi Click, a lesbian church member who helped organize a group called Fort Worth Via Media, which believes there should be room in the church for gay bishops. "You just can't compare them."

Liberals also point out that though Jesus never mentioned homosexuality, he did condemn divorce. They wonder why, since the church found a way to change its teaching on divorce, it can't do the same with homosexuality. Conservatives counter that the Bible is far from univocal on divorce. Mark (10:5–12) and Luke (16:16–18) say no exceptions, but Matthew (19:1–9 and 5:31–32) and Paul (1 Corinthians 7:10–16) do allow for circumstances where divorce is permissible, leaving the church enough scriptural wiggle room to change its position. Liberals point to biblical condemnations of everything from a man speaking against his father to sex during menstruation, eating bloody meat, tattooing, and wearing clothes of blended fabric. Why arbitrarily insist on a literal interpretation of a handful of Scripture passages in a church that is proudly and conspicuously non-fundamentalist? Conservative Episcopalians answer that this line of reasoning confuses civil and ritual law with moral law. Such prohibitions represent Old Testament civil law and are therefore not in force, says the conservative side: the Ten Commandments are in force, as are other moral pronouncements, such as those on homosexuality. And many liberals simply contend that because Jesus was loving and inclusive and forgiving and taught his followers to love one another, singling out gays as a special class of sinners is contrary to that love. Conservatives would say that homosexuals are not a special class of sinners. They are sinners, period, like everyone else. Conservatives also point out that Jesus did not welcome everyone unconditionally; he upheld the moral law of the Old Testament and could be a tough, demanding master. He would have loved and forgiven gays, they say. He also would have insisted that they repent of their sin.

Forced to Choose Sides

Perhaps the most pernicious effect of the General Convention's votes was that they forced Episcopalians to take sides. The result was to tear congregations apart, sometimes pitting members against each other, sometimes pitting them against their own clergy. Even in an overwhelmingly conservative parish like Roseberry's, the votes produced dissenting voices. A member of Christ Church's congregation, J.K. Ivey, was so disturbed by Roseberry's reaction to the General Convention that he wrote a letter of resignation. "Each time I open my mailbox," he wrote, "there is another 'hate-gram' from my beloved church that I no longer recognize. . . . You have posted several documents on line and by mail that call upon all members of Christ Church to 'Reject any position or policy of lifestyle which is contrary to scripture.'. . . Please let me know when you plan to advocate stoning, burning at the stake, and otherwise inflicting the death penalty, as required for some 87 different sins (homosexuality excluded)." Roseberry replied, "I must make a simple statement. The General Convention has erred in electing a man who cannot uphold the historical teaching of the Christian Church. Whether he is a homosexual or not is beside the point. . . . Your letter characterizes me as arrogant, judgmental, intolerant, and condemning. This is the same spirit of hate that you accuse me of." Ivey says he received "tons of hate mail" after his letter was posted on the Internet. "At first it ran 80–20 hate-to-good," he says. "Then at some point it reversed."

That sort of polarity made it harder for Episcopalians to do what they have long been famous for: finding common ground between extremes. Church members even use the Latin term for it: "via media"—"the middle way." It dates to Elizabeth I, who managed to hold Papists and Puritans together in the sixteenth century by insisting that they use a Book of Common Prayer while allowing wide latitude for personal beliefs. "A lot of people feel they are being forced to take a position they are not ready to take," says Father Chuck Treadwell, the rector of St. Peter's Episcopal Church in McKinney, whose congregation is mostly conservative. "They feel they are being drawn into a battle they don't necessarily want to fight." Treadwell was a delegate to the convention and voted against Robinson but was unhappy that the church had forced the issue. He shared his feelings with his church. "When I spoke to the issue, I came out of the pulpit and said, I do not know what the mind of God is. We were open; we talked about it. I did a lot of one-on-one counseling. Three families left because of it." . . .

Seeking Compromise

In Houston, conservative bishop Don A. Wimberly voted against consecrating Robinson's ordination and then wrote a letter to everyone in the diocese saying so, which angered many liberals. He then did something that many of his conservative counterparts elsewhere found difficult or impossible; He said he was not going to make an issue out of it. There would be no gay ordinations in his diocese and no same-sex blessings. But there would be room for everyone in the church. "I am not throwing people out and showing them the door," says Wimberly. "This is my understanding of Scripture, and it is the way I approach it. But that doesn't keep me from loving you or welcoming you into the community." When he visited liberal churches and was asked about his position, he explained it. At the annual diocesan council, in February, Wimberly's approach was to defuse the issue by urging delegates not to vote on whether to condemn the national church. "If I had not learned anything else at General Convention," he says. "I learned that when you vote, there are winners and losers. I said, 'I don't want the diocese to divide itself up like that.'" He says that he has received more than one thousand e-mails since Robinson's election—both for and against the church's position. But even with Wimberly's conciliatory approach, there are casualties. A recent one was the Reverend Paul Fromberg, a gay priest who chose to leave as rector of St. Andrew's Episcopal Church, in the Heights in Houston. Fromberg, who is heading to San Francisco, told the *Houston Chronicle*, "It is easier to be gay and a priest in the Diocese of California than it is in the Diocese of Texas."

In impoverished Africa, Anglicans are so exercised about this issue that entire provinces are no longer accepting donations from some American churches.

A few miles away from Wimberly's diocesan headquarters, at the 2,700-meter Palmer Memorial Episcopal Church, in Houston, Father Jim Nutter struggled to arrive at his own version of via media. As a convention delegate when the resolution was presented, Nutter had voted against Robinson, though he says he found the whole idea of the vote "political, arrogant, unilateral, and a huge disappointment." He returned to Houston to a congregation that was deeply torn and addressed the subject from the pulpit on August 17. "The issue before us is not whether we are going to have gay priests and bishops," he told them in his sermon. "You do know that, don't you? . . . The issue is not whether we are going to accept them. We have. The issue is this . . . Are we going to move from tacit acceptance to explicit approval and support?" He then confessed his own mixed feelings, explaining that the priest who had sent him to seminary was gay, his two favorite professors at seminary were gay, and a priest who had been his spiritual mentor was gay. He also staked out a middle ground. "The conservatives, for the most part, are not pharisaical homophobes," he said. "That language needs to stop! The liberals, for the most part, are not a bunch of New Age flakes, soft on Jesus, soft on Scripture. And that kind of language needs to stop." Like Roseberry, but for entirely different reasons, he got a standing ovation that Sunday. He says it amazed him.

But Nutter says that a "firestorm" broke after an October meeting where, for the first time, he told his congregation that he had voted no to Robinson but that, as he says, "after twenty years with this issue, I think I can get there from here—to support and ordain a practicing homosexual and to somehow bless same-sex marriages." He points to a nearly foot-high stack of printouts of e-mail he received on the subject. "God, I had despair that week," he says. "When I look back, I realize I was caught by surprise by the pain that people spilled out. All sorts of pain. There were liberals who said. 'How could you vote no? You had an agenda. You lied. You've been duplicitous. You have betrayed us." In the end, he says that only 20 people out of 2,700 left Palmer Memorial. The church's membership has actually increased, as have financial contributions.

Trying to Prevent a Split

In the loose confederation of dioceses that is the Episcopal Church of the United States of America, bishops wield enormous power. In Fort Worth, for example, Jack Iker is the chairman of the board of a corporation that owns all the lands, buildings, and financial resources of the diocese. He is elected by the clergy in his diocese. No matter how much presiding bishop Frank Griswold may dislike Iker's theology, there is very little he can do about it. Iker does not serve at his pleasure. And if Iker, or his compatriot James Stranton, in Dallas, chooses to try to break away and form a separate linkage to the Anglican Church, there may be little the denomination can do to stop him, particularly if the Archbishop of Canterbury approves it. There would be lawsuits, to be sure. The national church might try to claim the lands of Fort Worth's 56 congregations. Iker, of course, would likely have most of the world's 73 million Anglicans behind him. For now, Iker and Stanton and their dioceses are part of the Network, seeking realignment within the church, but there is always the threat that the twelve dissident bishops could pick up their toys and and go home.

The more immediate problem is how to handle individual conservative churches who find themselves unhappily saddled with bishops who voted for Gene Robinson. Here the spiritual and temporal sides of the church are already colliding—again, because of the awesome power of bishops. In St. Louis, Missouri, when the Church of the Good Shepherd voted to break away and affiliate with the Anglican Mission in America, the diocese sued it for its land and buildings. A non-jury trial is scheduled for this month. Last winter in Florida, two congregations voted to leave the church; one abandoned its property and buildings, and the other one was sued. These are just a few examples, but they underscore the church's main problem, which is how to keep dissident churches on board. . . .

The Network is still withholding money from the national church and seems more recalcitrant than ever. In impoverished Africa, Anglicans are so exercised about this issue that entire provinces are no longer accepting donations from some American churches. This is an astonishing and completely unexpected development. In March the newly consecrated bishop of New Hampshire could confidently state, "Some primates are declaring themselves in a state of impaired communion, but the fact of the matter is they're not sending our missionaries home. They haven't stopped cashing our checks." On April 15, however, Anglican archbishops from Africa said they would reject donations from any diocese that recognizes gay clergy and recommended giving the Episcopal Church three months to repent.

All of which leaves a global church with an apparently insoluble problem and millions of members holding their collective breath. "I have no idea what will happen," says Roseberry. "And I say that if you are not concerned about this issue, then you don't understand it."

13

Hare Krishnas Face Discrimination in America

Michael Kress

Michael Kress is a freelance writer based in Cambridge, Massachusetts.

Admittedly, the abuse that took place in the gurukulas (schools established by Hare Krishnas) is inexcusable. But more than a decade after these schools were closed and organizations were established to protect children, the International Society for Krishna Consciousness (ISKCON) still faces discrimination in America and worries it must continue to forsake traditional beliefs and adopt Western practices in order to survive.

From the beginning, Hare Krishnas faced hostility, as Americans took one look at their youth robed and shaved and cried "cult." Ironically, it was partly ISKCON's [International Society for Krishna Consciousness] fidelity to tradition that made Americans uncomfortable; while other Eastern transplants—such as Transcendental Meditation—did not demand major lifestyle changes, [A. C. Bhaktivedanta Swami] Prabhupada's followers fully embraced an Indian religion and culture.

"Dancing in the streets with okra robes on your men, women in saris with the red dot on their forehead, and reciting in Bengali old Krishna stories that originate from the 16th century is absolutely deemed to be cultic," asserts Larry Shinn,

Michael Kress, "Hare Krishna Comes of Age," *USA Today Magazine*, vol. 134, July 2005. Copyright © 2005 Society for the Advancement of Education. Reproduced by permission.

president of Berea College and author of *Dark Lord: Cult Images and the Hare Krishnas in America*. "But the 'strange' behavior is really Indian and Hindu. It's not some aberrant human being who's developed this system in the last 10 or 15 years."

Despite the success of those heady early days, ISKCON's problems were germinating even then. Suddenly living chaste and temperate lives under the authority of a guru was difficult, especially since so many converts were refugees from the sex-and-drugs counterculture. Some became involved in illegal activities. Despite Prabhupada's progressivism, some refused to initiate women, railed against female sexuality, and were abusive to women and children. In addition, ISKCON was, to a large extent, a victim of its own success.

"I don't think Prabhupada was expecting the movement to explode the way it did, and it did. So you had one elderly swami and the next thing, you had tens of thousands of disciples. Who's going to manage all those people?" asks Edwin Bryant, a professor of religion at Rutgers University and co-editor of *The Hare Krishna Movement: The Postcharismatic Fate of a Religious Transplant*. "Kids that were one minute smoking pot and living hedonistic lifestyles, the next minute they were shaved up and they were temple presidents."

Prabhupada "left the planet"—a Hare Krishna euphemism for death—in 1977, as the movement was still expanding. Instead of appointing a successor, he left ISKCON in the hands of a coterie of gurus known as the Governing Body Commission (GBC). Leadership struggles and misbehavior throughout the 1980s led to ISKCON's first major exodus. That also was when devotees began moving out of the temples en masse— for marriage and jobs, and because ISKCON's financial problems made supporting large numbers of monks unfeasible.

Though undertaken for pragmatic reasons, Anuttama [Dasa, ISKCON spokesman] says the move to "householders" —family-oriented congregations—actually represents a return to Caitanya's [15th-century Bengali monk] original ideals, which never called for large-scale renunciation. Ultimately, the householder trend would be considered the most important factor in ISKCON's survival and a sign that it truly refocused its values after the dark days of scandal and tragedy. Valuing the nuclear family may not seem revolutionary, but to many early devotees, children were little more than a distraction. "Dump the load and hit the road," went a saying about pregnant women in ISKCON.

Abusing the Children

Take Ananda Tiller, for example. Born in 1975 to Hare Krishna parents, Tiller started at the Dallas gurukula (boarding school) when she was four. Her father was the community's head priest, but he had little interaction with Ananda and her brother. Their mother was off proselytizing and made only occasional visits. At the gurukulas, students encountered a rigorous curriculum of religious instruction, and Tiller says she learned to write her name in Sanskrit before English. Teachers—entirely untrained—railed against the evils of the outside world, with which children had few encounters.

Tiller endured physical, emotional, and sexual abuse. "As a child, my body, mind, soul—everything—was given to this God and given to these people, and they took it all, even my six-year-old body," she relates.

In 1986, Tiller and her brother switched to public school. There, she was terrified, encountering the things her teachers had warned about. "It was extremely confusing," she recalls of the transition. "We really never left that city block when we were in Dallas, and all we knew was that in the outside world were these devilish meat-eaters that were going to poison our minds."

Tiller's teen years were filled with drugs, sex, and suicide attempts. Other gurukula alumni are homeless and some have committed suicide. Today, Tiller is the mother of two and has been working to recover from the trauma, though it is a daily struggle.

Part of moving on, in her eyes, was joining a $400,000,000 lawsuit brought against ISKCON by nearly 100 former gurukula students. At first unsure she wanted to take part, Tiller visited the Dallas temple in 2001 for the first time in 15 years. "These memories just started flooding me. I became very bitter and wanted to see some changes."

ISKCON officials insist they are working not just to salvage temples but to do right by the victims.

Internal Control

Krishna leaders claim those changes already have occurred. By the time the suit was filed, ISKCON had been reeling from the scandal for a decade, since the first whispers about abuse in the gurukulas began circulating in the early 1990s. In 1996, a group of alumni made a presentation to the GBC describing their experiences and, around that time, the last of the North American gurukulas was closed.

ISKCON established two organizations in response to the revelations. Children of Krishna offers support and financial compensation to victims; it has distributed about $250,000. The Child Protection Office has three purposes: investigation and adjudication of abuse allegations; grants to victims; and establishing awareness and protection programs in ISKCON temples and schools.

In an unusual step, the editor of an official ISKCON publication asked [Middlebury College professor Burke] Rochford to write an article documenting the abuse. The piece was published in 1999 and, before long, ISKCON's voluntary revelation of the horrors that took place in its schools became international news. The lawsuit was filed soon after.

Insisting they have nowhere near the $400,000,000 demanded by the suit—a claim scholars confirmed—several of the temples filed for Chapter 11 bankruptcy protection, which allowed them to negotiate a settlement of the lawsuit while ensuring the temples retain enough funds to stay open. As part of the process, ISKCON invited any abused gurukula alumni to submit a claim, and about 400 came forward, on top of the 100 named in the lawsuit.

It will take years for ISKCON to move past the tragedy fully, just as it will take a lifetime for the victims to feel whole again.

ISKCON officials insist they are working not just to salvage temples but to do right by the victims. "As individual devotees, and as parents, and as elders, and as an institution, we bear a tremendous moral responsibility to help these kids," Anuttama reasons.

Critics, though, say the changes do not run deep enough. "There are some really wonderful, smart, liberal people who were always jumping up and down saying that something had to be done," suggests Maria Ekstrand, a longtime Hare Krishna and Bryant's co-editor. "But the only reason the rest of them listened was out of fear of what would happen if they didn't."

Modeled after Indian boarding schools, the gurukulas were supposed to create a new generation of committed Hare Krishnas, but the schools failed their children in a tragic way. "They were going to be the future leaders," Bryant says. "Instead, the vast, vast, vast majority all left."

Still Dealing with the Past

Today, the gurukulas are closed, abandoned in favor of a more Western model: Sunday schools and day schools. Family and home have replaced mission and temple as the center of Hare Krishna life.

ISKCON gets credit from observers for dealing proactively with the tragedy once it was revealed. At the same time, though, the attorney spearheading the lawsuit, a veteran of abuse suits against institutions, including the Catholic Church, says the abuse described by gurukula alumni is the worst he has encountered. It will take years for ISKCON to move past the tragedy fully, just as it will take a lifetime for the victims to feel whole again.

"Child Protection Office Closing!" The article, written by the head of the office, appears on a Hare Krishna website and blames "tens of thousands of dollars in unfulfilled pledges" for the demise of the six-year-old office. I ask Anuttama about it. He says he has funds saved for the office and is fund-raising aggressively to keep it open. "I will die before that office closes," he insists.

Though a false alarm, the office has seen its budget shrink yearly. Nevertheless, it has investigated about 300 alleged abusers, and adjudicated about 100 cases. Punishments include banishment from leadership positions, restitution, and writing apology letters. Lately, the office has focused mostly on running healing seminars for abused children and developing prevention programs. While praising the office for its sincere efforts, critics see the process as inherently flawed.

"The GBC is trying to police itself, which never really works in an organization," Ekstrand charges. "If you are accused of doing these horrible things, I think the only thing to do is open up and allow professional outsiders to investigate what happened, let them make decisions based on their investigation, and let those decisions stand."

She says that the Child Protection Office's decisions are not always followed, and that the office is not empowered to mete out severe punishments, such as perpetual banishment from positions of spiritual leadership. If an abuser truly repents, Ekstrand says, "You should probably go and wash dishes and clean toilets and show that you're really humble and you regret things."

To most Hare Krishnas, the abuse tragedy is not an everyday presence. Krishnas I encountered expressed several responses to the scandals: many religions have to deal with abuse, so ISKCON is not unique; it is in the past and ISKCON has eradicated it; the perpetrators were acting against Krishna's true teachings.

I also found another reaction best summed up in the words of Mangala-Arotick Dasi, a 28-year-old convert who lives with her husband near the Boston temple: "I feel responsible. Just by aligning myself with this society, and with this group, I've voluntarily taken on that experience, that identity, and that responsibility." . . .

The Challenges Ahead

Nitai [an elder statesman at the Boston temple, Nimai] dreams of creating a fully American ISKCON, one that does not look to India for names, clothing, food, and liturgy. "If we are to have a future—and I believe we are—then we have to adopt forms that are more consonant with Western styles." Listening to him muse about the future, it was easy to forget the challenges threatening ISKCON. For one thing, as his story shows, ISKCON and Krishna-consciousness no longer are synonymous. Schismatic groups are siphoning off ISKCON members, while many individuals worship privately, without temple affiliation. "The tradition has taken root here, but the more time that goes by, it seems that ISKCON does not have a monopoly anymore," Ekstrand observes.

Additionally, a major demographics problem looms. Though I met several dedicated young people in Boston, new converts are few in number, and missionary activity no longer is a priority. The children of early converts mostly have fled the movement, scarred by their gurukula experiences.

One source of vitality for ISKCON has been Indian immigrants, without whom many temples would be in serious trouble. In some places, ISKCON offers the only Hindu worship, but even given options, many Indians choose ISKCON. The movement, though, remains run almost entirely by white converts and, in many temples, the two groups do not mix much. "We may have, in time, the very curious possibility of having a largely East Indian congregation with white-faced Westerners preaching and serving on the altar in Hindu temples. . . ." Rochford surmises.

Battles rage on many fronts: the role of women; denominational authority vs. local autonomy; the limits of dissent; the abuse and its aftermath.

Even in ISKCON's much-praised move to householders, Bryant sees a problem: Without monks, who will maintain the temples? Already, many American temples have brought priests from other countries to oversee worship. ISKCON, Bryant says, has failed to produce charismatic individuals who can lead by the example of their high spiritual attainment and bring in new converts. "Ultimately, people want to see," he offers. "They don't just want to hear philosophy."

Then there are finances. Bookselling, once the movement's economic backbone, no longer provides substantial income. Communities rely solely on donations and, Rochford indicates, "They're struggling in most every instance to get by."

An American Problem

That is true in North America only. Abroad ISKCON is thriving—especially in India, where the Hindu movement founded for Westerners is surprisingly popular. Bryant suggests that, for Indians eager to Westernize, ISKCON offers a bridge between past and present, traditional religion imported from the coveted West. Even there, though, all is not well. When it comes to child abuse awareness, Anuttama relates, "They're where we were 20 years ago"—which is to say, in denial. At least one American who oversaw a gurukula rife with abuse is rumored to be teaching in India. Anuttama says he tells Indian Hare Krishnas: "Don't make the same mistakes America went through. . . ."

Still, the movement's stunning new Indian temples attract political VIPs and religious pilgrims alike, while in the U.S., ISKCON hopes just to keep its existing temples open. "The future is going to be one of continual change, but I think it's going to be one where a movement that's already struggling, financially and otherwise, is likely to continue to struggle," Rochford reasons.

The struggle is not just for resources; the soul of ISKCON is at stake. Battles rage on many fronts: the role of women; denominational authority vs. local autonomy; the limits of dissent; the abuse and its aftermath. It would seem that the liberals are winning. More women than ever serve as leaders; websites feature vociferous debate on everything from theology to the lawsuit; and child abuse prevention is a clear priority. "But at the same time," Ekstrand warns, "there is a very strong fundamentalist contingent, and they are going to be fighting all of this tooth and nail."

For their part, ISKCON leaders are finding that doing the things an American religion does is not easy. Reaching the proper balance between institutionalization and expressive spirituality is a major challenge, contends Anuttama, who, like many, joined ISKCON to escape organized religion. "How do you address those broader needs of parking lots and playgrounds and marriage counseling but not lose the essential spirituality that inspires religious people?" he asks, offering an answer that centers around core ISKCON values.

"People become overwhelmed with wanting to possess more and own more and lust for power and economic exploitation. If we stay true to our principles, then we will be okay. But if we forget that and if it becomes just a superficial affiliation, then we can be in trouble."

Organizations to Contact

The editors have compiled the following list of organizations concerned with the issues debated in this book. The descriptions are derived from materials provided by the organizations. All have publications or information available for interested readers. The list was compiled on the date of publication of the present volume; the information provided here may change. Be aware that many organizations take several weeks or longer to respond to inquiries, so allow as much time as possible.

American Center for Law and Justice (ACLJ)
PO Box 90555, Washington, DC   20090-0555
(757) 226-2489 • fax: (757) 226-2836
Web site: www.aclj.org

The purpose of the ACLJ is to educate, promulgate, conciliate, and, where necessary, litigate, to ensure that the rights of religious freedom and freedom of speech are protected under the law.

American Civil Liberties Union (ACLU)
125 Broad St., 18th Floor, New York, NY   10004-2400
(888) 567-2258 • fax: (212) 549-2646
Web site: www.aclu.org

The ACLU works in the courts, legislatures, and communities to defend and preserve the individual rights and liberties guaranteed to all people in this country by the Constitution and laws of the United States.

American Jewish Committee (AJC)
PO Box 705, New York, NY   10150
(212) 751-4000 • Fax (212) 891-1492
Web site: www.ajc.org

The AJC works to combat anti-semitism and all forms of bigotry; promote pluralism and shared civic values; protect human rights and combat abuses; assert Israel's right to exist in peace and security with its neighbors; and safeguard and strengthen Jewish life.

Americans United for the Separation of Church and State (AU)
518 C St. NE, Washington, DC   20002
(202) 466-3234 • fax: (202) 466-2587
Web site: www.au.org

Americans United defends separation of church and state in the courts, educates legislators, works with the media to inform Americans about religious freedom issues, and organizes local chapters all over the country.

Coalition Against Religious Discrimination
Onty Hileman, Executive Director
(202) 238-9088 • fax: (202) 238-9003
e-mail: info@stopreligiousdiscrimination.com
Web site: www.stopreligiousdiscrimination.com

The Coalition Against Religious Discrimination is a network of nearly seventy religious, civil rights, labor, health, and advocacy organizations that oppose the "faith-based initiative" and other efforts to allow federal tax dollars to fund religious discrimination.

Council on American-Islamic Relations (CAIR)
453 New Jersey Ave. SE, Washington, DC   20003
(202) 488-8787 • fax: (202) 488-0833
e-mail: info@cair.com
Web site: www.cair-net.org

CAIR's mission is to enhance understanding of Islam, encourage dialogue, protect civil liberties, empower American Muslims, and build coalitions that promote justice and mutual understanding.

Duncan Black Macdonald Center for Christian-Muslim Relations
Macdonald Center, Hartford Seminary, Hartford, CT   06105
(860) 509-9534 • fax: (860) 509-9539
Web site: http://macdonald.hartsem.edu

All Macdonald Center faculty and personnel are committed to the importance of better understanding between and among faiths, and to supporting efforts toward building relationships based on tolerance and trust.

Family Research Council (FRC)
801 G St. NW, Washington, DC   20001
(202) 393-2100 • fax: (202) 393-2134
Web site: www.frc.org

The FRC shapes public debate and formulates public policy that values human life and upholds the institutions of marriage and the family. The FRC promotes the Judeo-Christian worldview as the basis for a just, free, and stable society.

Religious Action Center of Reform Judaism (RAC)
Arthur and Sara Jo Kobacker Building
Washington, DC   20036
(202) 387-2800
Web site: http://rac.org

The RAC educates and mobilizes the American Jewish community on legislative and social concerns as an advocate in Congress on issues ranging from Israel and Soviet Jewry to economic justice; from civil rights to international peace and religious liberty.

Unitarian Universalist Association of Congregations: Washington Office for Advocacy (UUA)
1320 18th St. NW, Suite 300B, Washington, DC   20036
(202) 296-4672 • fax: (202) 296-4673
Web site: www.uua.org

The Unitarian Universalist Association supports the separation of church and state in relation to public education, partisan politics, free exercise and religious pluralism, and encourages the maintenance of a public education system free of religious influence including prayer in schools and the inclusion of creationism in scientific textbooks.

Bibliography

Books

Geneive Abdo
Mecca and Main Street: Muslim Life in America after 9/11. New York: Oxford University Press, 2006.

Elliott Abrams
Faith or Fear: How Jews Can Survive in a Christian America. New York: Simon & Schuster, 1997.

Carol Barner-Barry
Contemporary Paganism: Minority Religions in a Majoritarian America. New York: Palgrave Macmillan, 2005.

Stephen L. Carter
God's Name in Vain: The Wrongs and Rights of Religion in Politics. New York: Basic Books, 2000.

Jocelyne Cesari
When Islam and Democracy Meet. New York: Palgrave Macmillan, 2004.

Diana Eck
A New Religious America: How a "Christian Country" Has Now Become the World's Most Religiously Diverse Nation. New York: HarperCollins, 2001.

Aladdin Elaasar
Silent Victims: The Plight of Arab & Muslim Americans in Post 9/11 America. Bloomington, IN: AuthorHouse, 2004.

David Hackett, ed.
Religion and American Culture. New York: Routledge, 2nd ed., 2003.

Israr Hasan   *Muslims in America: What Everyone*
                       Needs to Know. Bloomington, IN:
                       AuthorHouse, 2006.

Arshad Khan   *Islam, Muslims, and America: Under-*
                       standing the Basis of Their Conflict.
                       New York: Algora, 2003.

Isaac Kramnick   *The Godless Constitution: A Moral*
and R. Laurence   *Defense of the Secular State.* New
Moore   York: W.W. Norton, 2005.

David Limbaugh   *Persecution: How Liberals Are Waging*
                       War Against Christianity. Washington,
                       DC: Regnery, 2003.

Phillip Lucas and   *New Religious Movements in the 21⁰*
Thomas Robbins,   *Century.* New York: Routledge, 2004.
eds.

Barbara McGraw   *Taking Religious Pluralism Seriously:*
and Jo Formicola,   *Spiritual Politics on America's Sacred*
eds.   *Ground.* Waco, TX: Baylor University
                       Press, 2005.

J. Judd Owen   *Religion and the Demise of Liberal*
                       Rationalism: The Foundational Crisis
                       of the Separation of Church and State.
                       Chicago: University of Chicago Press,
                       2001.

Henri Picciotto   *Reframing Anti-Semitism: Alternate*
and Mitchell   *Jewish Perspectives.* Oakland, CA: Jew-
Plitnick, eds.   ish Voice for Peace, 2004.

Alan Sears and   *ACLU vs. America: Exposing the*
Craig Osten   *Agenda to Redefine Moral Values.*
                       Nashville, TN: Broadman & Holman,
                       2005.

Jay Sekulow   *America v. God: Why We Must Re-*
                       verse the Assault on Faith in Our
                       Courts. San Francisco: Harper, 2007.

Jane I. Smith   *Islam in America.* New York: Colum-
                       bia University Press, 1999.

Steven Smith   *Getting over Equality: A Critical Diag-*
                       nosis of Religious Freedom in America.
                       New York: New York University
                       Press, 2001.

Mathew Staver   *Eternal Vigilance: Knowing and Pro-*
                       tecting Your Religious Freedom. Nash-
                       ville, TN: Broadman & Holman,
                       2005.

Mark Weldon   *The Myth of Christian America: What*
Whitten   *You Need to Know About the Separa-*
                       tion of Church and State. Macon, GA:
                       Smyth and Helwys, 1999.

Periodicals

Eric Alterman   "Neocon Dreams, American Night-
                       mares," *Nation*, August 28, 2006.

Emily Bazar   "Trimming 'Christmas' from Trees
                       Stirs Debate," *USA Today*, December
                       1, 2005.

Rod Dreher   "Christmas Bombing," *National Re-*
                       view, December 31, 2002.

Roger Ebert   "Public Prayer Fanatics Borrow Page
                       from Enemy's Script," *Chicago Sun-*
                       Times, March 5, 2003.

T. Jeremy Gunn	"A fictional 'War on Christmas,'" *USA Today*, December 18, 2005.
David Alan Hart	"Preventing Conflict by Understanding Islam," *World & I*, February 2005.
Lawrence Jablecki	"A Critique of Faith-Based Prison Programs," *Humanist*, September–October 2005.
David Limbaugh	"Florida School District Bans Choir from Church," *Human Events*, September 23, 2002.
Paula Martina	"Blunt-Force Trauma," *Lesbian News*, January 2005.
Natalie Hope McDonald	"The Hypocritical Oath," *Advocate*, April 11, 2006.
Mark Pinsky	"Southern Jews and Evangelicals: Coming Together," *USA Today*, August 7, 2006.
Daniel Pipes	"America's Muslims Against America's Jews," *Commentary*, May 1, 1999.
Ramesh Ponnuru	"Secularism and Its Discontents," *National Review*, December 27, 2004.
Sarah Pulliam	"Military Culture War," *Christianity Today*, April 2006.
Laura Putre	"Amazing Grace and Resolve," *Advocate*, February 19, 2002.
Matthew Rothschild	"Cheap Slurs," *Progressive*, October 2006.

Alan Singer   "Separation of Church and State Pro-
                   tects Both Secular and Religious
                   Worlds," *Phi Delta Kappan*, February
                   2000.

Ben Stein   "America Bipolarized," *American
                   Spectator*, June 2006.

Chris Weinkopf   "Cheering the Code After Punching
                   the Passion," *American Enterprise*,
                   June 2006.

Jack Wertheimer   "Judaism and the Future of Religion
                   in America: The Situation of Conser-
                   vative Judaism Today," *Judaism*,
                   Summer–Fall 2005.

Index